SIR RICHARD BLACKMORE AND THE WITS

A Study of
"Commendatory Verses on the Author of the Two
Arthurs and the Satyr against Wit" (1700)

RICHARD C. BOYS

1969
OCTAGON BOOKS
New York

PR3318
B5
B6
1969

To
MY MOTHER AND FATHER

"*Parnassus* is in Arms against it self."

—William Ayloffe

PREFACE

THIS study is in no way meant to be an attempt to "rescue" Sir Richard Blackmore's reputation, as Dr. Johnson thought he was doing in the *Lives of the Poets*. Perhaps posterity has dealt with Blackmore more harshly than he deserves, perhaps not. At any rate, few people today, even in the light of a reawakened interest in the City Bard, are concerned with Blackmore *per se*. At least one scholar sees in Blackmore a symbol of social ferment and approaches him in this spirit. While some attention is paid to social forces in this book, I have placed the emphasis on *Commendatory Verses* as the center of a literary quarrel.

My task has been made easier and more pleasant by the kindness of several scholars. Professor Louis I. Bredvold and Professor John Arthos, of the University of Michigan, and Professor Horace A. Eaton, of Syracuse University, were gracious enough to read the manuscript and make invaluable suggestions. Professor Raymond D. Havens, of the Johns Hopkins University, as always, gave unstintingly of his time and assistance; he also lent me the first three editions of the *Satyr against Wit*. It is my sincere hope that Professor Havens will realize how grateful his students are for the help they have received from him, in the classroom and out. From the work of two scholars who had already given much thought to the problems of *Commendatory Verses*, Professor Edward N. Hooker, of the University of California at Los Angeles, and Professor Benjamin Boyce, of Nebraska University, I have gained immeasurably. Each read the manuscript with care, and each passed on to me information which made my task considerably lighter. I am also indebted to Mr. William Jackson, of the Houghton Library, Harvard, for several favors; to Dr. John Gordan, Curator of the New York Public Library's Berg Collection; to Captain Robert M. Krapp; and to Professor V. de Sola Pinto, of Nottingham University, whose researches into the life and works of Sedley led him into the middle of the whirlpool caused by *Commendatory Verses*. Last of all, while he did not have a hand directly in the preparation of this book, the late Arthur E. Case's help should not go unnoticed, for he first introduced me to *Commendatory Verses*. Over a period of ten years he was a good friend and a thoughtful adviser. He will be missed by all friends of eighteenth-century literature.

A small but timely grant from the Horace H. Rackham Fund made possible the purchase of photostats of *Discommendatory Verses* needed for this work.

R. C. B.

The University of Michigan
Ann Arbor

CONTENTS

APPENDIXES

NOTE

The following condensed forms of reference are used:

Dennis, ed. Hooker = *Critical Works of John Dennis*, ed. Edward N. Hooker (Baltimore, 1939, 1943).

Harlow, *Christopher Codrington* = Vincent T. Harlow, *Christopher Codrington* (Oxford, 1928).

Johnson, *Lives of the Poets* = Samuel Johnson, *Lives of the English Poets*, ed. G. B. Hill (Oxford, 1905).

Works of Dryden, ed. Scott-Saintsbury = *Works of John Dryden*, ed. Sir Walter Scott and George Saintsbury (Edinburgh, 1882).

I. THE BACKGROUND

THE spring of the year 1700 reflected more than the after-glow of one century and the dawn of another; in May the great Dryden died, and with him went some of the literary turbulence of the Restoration. Not that life on Parnassus was destined to be peaceful and calm — far from it. Literary activity (and the Augustan age was certainly active) invariably meant literary dissension, as the quarrels of Pope, Swift, Addison, and others show. Only a few years later one writer, William Ayloffe, was complaining bitterly of this bickering:

> The Age, of late, has been so pester'd with Miscellanies, that the Press ran as great a Risque of being ungrateful to Mankind (not to call it a Nusance) as from those intolerable Crowds of Pamphlets, which are every Day obtruded upon us; Such a Glut of Verse and Prose, that, what with indifferent Authors mercenary and partial Pens, scandalous Libels, and abominable Panegyrics, one wou'd almost forswear reading any thing that is New, to prevent the Miseries of Disappointment. *Parnassus* is in Arms against it self, and the Daughters of *Helicon* as mutinous as the execrable Sons of the Earth. The Factious Ensigns are every where display'd, and the Various Wits rank'd in formidable Batallions. If a Man sets up for a Poet, he is Immediately attacqu'd by a Satyrical Party; Destruction is the Word; and, as for Quarter, they give none: These are the Blood-thirsty Hussars of *Parnassus*, cut out for the Ruin of others, tho' rarely with any great Honour to themselves. Whence comes it (Gentlemen) that such Civil Dissensions harrass the Castalian Plains? Does not every Chocolate-house furnish you with Matter enough for your pointed Wits? And are there not Follies and Vices enough in Mankind, but you must traduce one the other? [1]

[1] Preface to the *Poetical Works of the Honourable Sir Charles Sedley, Baronet* (1707), pp. i-ii.

1

One altercation which bridges the gap between the Age of Dryden and the Age of Pope has received far less attention than its importance warrants. In the battle which surrounds the publication of the far from complimentary poetical miscellany, *Commendatory Verses on the Author of the Two Arthurs and the Satyr Against Wit*, By Some of His Particular Friends (1700), Sir Richard Blackmore, the champion of piety and "decency," was beset by the "frivolous" Wits of his day, who were evidently unaware of the truth of Dr. Johnson's sage remark that "a man who tells me my play is very bad, is less my enemy than he who lets it die in silence." [2] The effects of this fight were far-reaching, since before it was over most of the leading literary figures of the time were involved. The immediate battle span was seven years, from 1695 to 1702, but echoes were resounding from Helicon as late as the *Dunciad* quarrel, twenty-six years later.

Early in 1695 a long poem in the heroic manner, *Prince Arthur*, was presented to the public, the first of Blackmore's "incessant discharge of epics." [3] Since Blackmore's poetry has from the beginning been a favorite hunting ground for scoffers seeking poetic cauliflowers, it is useless to labor the point here. The following passages from *Prince Arthur* will serve to illustrate the atrocious verse:

> Flashes of Fire from his red Eyeballs flow'd,
> Like Lightning breaking from a lowring Cloud.
> So when a Toad, squat on a Border spies,
> The Gardner passing by, his bloodshot Eyes
> With Spite, and Rage inflam'd, dart Fire around
> The verdant Walks, and on the flowry Ground,
> The bloated Vermin loathsome Poison spits,
> And swoln and bursting with his Malice sits.

> (Bk. VI, p. 177)

---

[2] *Boswell's Journal of a Tour to the Hebrides*, ed. F. A. Pottle and C. H. Bennett (New York, 1936), p. 238.

[3] G. L. Craik, *Compendious History of English Literature* (London, 1861), II, 235. *Prince Arthur* was advertised in the Term Catalogue for February.

> These Breasts she empties with her Infant Jaws,
> I File her Teeth, and Shape her tender Claws.
> I Nurse her on the horrid Alps high Tops,
> And feed her hunger with *Cerberean* Sops
> Dipt in *Tartarean* Gall, and Hemlock Juice,
> That in her Veins will noble Blood produce.
> Fierce Tygers, Dragons, Wolves about her stay,
> They grin, and snap, and bite, and snarling play.
>
> (Bk. I, p. 20)

These excerpts and such a strenuous line as

> The lab'ring Mounts Belch drossy Vomit out
>
> (Bk. III, p. 67)

demonstrate Blackmore's particular fondness for the horrific, in which he is at his worst. There are many such passages in Blackmore's epics, but there are more in which the worst offense is mediocrity.

From the start the poet invited trouble, for he was a perfect target for the Wits. He soon learned that:

> If, on *Parnassus'* Top you sit,
> You rarely bite, are always bit:
> Each Poet of inferior Size
> On you shall rail and criticize;
> And strive to tear you Limb from Limb,
> While others do as much for him.[4]

For one thing, the naïveté of the aspiring poet (which later became a kind of martyred determination) is incredible. In the Preface to *King Arthur* Blackmore tells us that he wrote *Prince Arthur* solely for his own amusement, the relaxation of a tired doctor. Nor did he pretend to careful workmanship and polish:

> . . . The greatest part of that *Poem* was written in *Coffee-houses*, and in passing up and down the Streets; because I had little leisure elsewhere to apply to it. Another reason of the Defects that appear in that

---

[4] "On Poetry: a Rapsody," in *The Poems of Jonathan Swift*, ed. Harold Williams (Oxford, 1937), II, 651.

wr[i]ting is this, That when I undertook it I had long been a stranger to the Muses. I had read but little *Poetry* throughout my whole Life, and in fifteen years before, I had not, as I can remember, wrote a hundred Lines in Verse, excepting a Copy of Latine Verses in honour of a Friend's Book (p. v).

Had he stopped here the Epick Poet might well have escaped with little more than a metric knuckle-rapping, a crushing Drydenian couplet of the sort whose sting Shadwell had felt. But Blackmore had a loftier purpose in mind when he wrote his poems, namely, to rescue literature from those writers who had debased it: "Our Poets seem engag'd in a general *Confederacy* to ruin the End of their own Art, to expose *Religion* and *Virtue*, and bring *Vice* and *Corruption of Manners* into Esteem and Reputation" (p. iv). For Blackmore it became a Crusade: "I was willing to make one *Effort* towards the rescuing the *Muses* out of the hands of these *Ravishers*, to restore them to their sweet and chast Mansions, and to engage them in an Employmeut [*sic*] suitable to their *Dignity*" (*Prince Arthur*, p. ix).

The storm clouds gathered, and if Blackmore wanted a Holy War he was to get one. As yet he was not sufficiently important — and hence not sufficiently dangerous — to warrant a blast from both barrels, the best that the Wits at Will's Coffee-house had to offer, but they jeered in the accepted fashion and called on a sober critic, John Dennis, to put an end to this nonsense once and for all. In many ways Dennis seems out of place among the Wits. He is above everything else a serious literary critic, possibly the best between Dryden and Johnson; the picture that has come down to us shows a querulous person, a man of strong principles, a little sour, who fights with almost everyone. It is hard to associate him with the gaiety and conviviality we usually think of in connection with Will's and the Wits. At any rate, after a careful analysis of *Prince Arthur* he produced, in 1696, his *Remarks on a Book Entituled, Prince Arthur*. Probably there was less malice in it than the men of Will's wanted, for it concerned itself solely with the effectiveness of *Prince Arthur* as an epic poem: " My intention was only to consider this Gentleman in his poetical capacity, and to make some Remarks upon the reasonableness of his Design and upon the felicity of his execution . . . . I intended to shew that Mr. *Blackmore's* Action has neither unity, nor integrity, nor morality, nor universality, and consequently that he can have no *Fable* and no *Heroick Poem* . . . and to shew that [the narration] is neither probable, delightful, nor wonderful." [5] Dennis was obviously the critical champion of the Wits; the *Remarks* were intended to demolish Blackmore for all time. Later he was again the mouthpiece for the Wits when he answered Collier's charges against the immorality of the stage.[6]

Blackmore saw in the Wits the instruments of evil, and in the Preface to *King Arthur* (1697) he turned his attention to them specifically (pp. i-ii) :

   . . . I must have been extreamly ignorant of the nature of Humane Passions, if I had not certainly foreseen, that not only the Design of the Poem, but likewise the *Provoking Preface* to it, must needs have engag'd a *Considerable Party*, among whom were several Men of Wit and Parts, to use their utmost Endeavour to sink its Reputation . . . .

   Besides, when I consider'd that I was so great a stranger to the Muses, and by no means free of the *Poets Company*, having never Kiss'd their Governour's hands, nor made the least Court to the Committee that sits in *Covent Garden*; and that therefore mine was not so much as a *Permission Poem*, but a pure, *downright Interloper*, it was but natural to conclude, that those Gentlemen, who by Assisting, Crying up, Excusing and Complementing one another, carry on their poetical Trade in a Joynt-stock, would certainly do what they could to sink and ruin an *unlicens'd Adventurer* . . . .

   Accordingly when the Poem came forth they attack'd it, tho' perhaps not with all the Discretion, yet with all the Fury Imaginable; But all their Strokes were lost, and all their Efforts made in vain . . . . For their Character and Temper, as well as the Grounds and Reasons of their Outcrys and Opposition were so well known, that they could by no means pass for unbyass'd and Disinterested Judges . . . .

With these words Blackmore let slip the dogs of war. Nor

---

[5] *Dennis*, ed. Hooker, I (1939), 52, 46.   [6] *Ibid.*, II (1943), xlix.

was it a mere skirmish to be forgotten overnight, for when Blackmore boasted that he had "never Kiss'd their Governour's hands" he threw down the gage at Dryden's feet. Blackmore did not mince words. In the Preface to *Prince Arthur* he went on to say that any man who "*lavish[es] out his* Life and Wit *in propagating* Vice and Corruption of Manners . . . *may he go off the Stage unpity'd,* complaining *of* Neglect *and* Poverty, *the just Punishments of his* Irreligion *and* Folly" (p. viii). In reply Dryden lashed back at Blackmore in a fury that seems out of proportion to the offense, when we consider that the assailant was a person of little consequence.[7]

Late in 1699 Blackmore again defied the Wits in his *Satyr against Wit,*[8] which, since it plays an important part in the battle of *Commendatory Verses,* is described in some detail below. The *Satyr* appeared with no poet's name on the title page, a ruse which fooled no one and which gave rise to a good deal of amused speculation on the part of the Wits:

[*Satyr against Wit*] came, like Melchisedeck into the World, without *Father* or *Mother;* I mean the *Author,* for several *Reasons* best known to himself, has not thought fit to set his *Name* before it: However, he is not so conceal'd as he fancies himself; for if there is any certainty in *Physiognomy,* or the Child to be known by the resembling the Features of his *Father,* as they say the *Austrian* Family are by the *Lip,* it was undoubtedly written by the *City Bard,* the same worthy Gentleman, who about three *Years* ago *lampoon'd K. William* in an *Heroic Poem,* by the same Token, that he was *Knighted* for it. I have been told he has disown'd the *Bastard* in several Companies, but that won't serve his turn: The *Grand Jury* at Will's have found the *Bill* against him; so now he must e'en take the *Brat* home, and bring it up in its *Father's Religion,* I mean, in *Hypocrisie* and *Backbiting.*[9]

---

[7] See below, pp. 13-17.

[8] The title page of the first edition is marked 1700, but Scott reports that Luttrell's copy is dated November 23, 1699 (*Works of Dryden,* ed. Scott-Saintsbury, I, 352; advertised in the *Post-Man,* issue of November 21-23, 1699).

[9] Tom Brown, "To Sir W. S——. Upon the two incomparable Poems, the Satyr against Wit, and the Poetae Britannici" (dated January 8, 1700 ?), in the *Works of . . . Voiture* (1705), 1701 section, pp. 127-128.

The greatest sin of the wicked men of Will's, the *Satyr*
asserts, is that they seek to undermine all virtue, private and
public, for they "crop each budding Virtue's tender head"
(p. 1); if they succeed, these loose, degenerate rakes will
completely destroy the whole state (p. 5). They are soft
and lacking in a "noble roughness" (p. 4), which has always
been England's heritage. Their wit is a form of insanity
which frequently resembles a fit (p. 4). Scornful of almost
everything that is good, the Wits threaten to demolish the
best in various branches of British culture and life. All true
learning is to them an object of scorn (p. 6) and they abhor
"right Reason" (p. 6). Their degrading influence is being
felt in all walks of life, even in the Church:

> Aloud the Church and Clergy they condemn,
> Curse all their Order, and their God blaspheme (p. 6).

> Let those Correction have, and not Applause,
> That Heav'n affront and ridicule its Laws.
> No sober Judge will Atheism e'er permit
> To pass for Sense, or Blasphemy for Wit (p. 12).

Literature, too, has felt their slimy touch, for Wit

> Has laid the Muses choicest Gardens wast,
> Broke their Inclosures and their Groves defac't (p. 8).

> Gardens and Groves *Parnassus* did adorn,
> Condemn'd to Thistles now, and curst with Thorn.
> Instead of Flowers and Herbs of wholsom use,
> It does rank Weeds and pois'nous Plants produce.
> Fitter to be for *Witches* a Retreat,
> *Owls, Satyrs, Monkies*, than the Muses Seat (p. 12).

Wit, in enticing young men away from their legitimate
studies, is the enemy of Law:

> Wit does enfeeble and debauch the Mind,
> Before to Business or to Arts inclin'd.
> How useless is a Sauntering empty Wit,
> Only to please with Jests at Dinner fit?
> What hopeful Youths for Bar and Bench design'd

> Seduced by Wit have learn'd *Coke* declin'd?
> For what has Wit to do with Sense or Law?
> Can that in Titles find or mend a Flaw? (p. 7).

Wit has, in fact, ruined the lives of many promising young men in all professions:

> In *G[arth]* the Wit the Doctor has undone,
> In *S[malwoo]d* the Divine, Heav'ns guard poor *Ad[di]son.*
> An able Senator is lost in *M[oy]l,*
> And a fine Scholar sunk by Wit in *B[oy]l* (p. 8).

The problem is, then,

> To regulate the Nation's Grievance, Wit . . . .
> If once the Muses Chequer would deny
> To take false Wit, 'twould lose its currency (p. 9).

To remedy this deplorable situation Blackmore calls on a group of noble lords to act as arbiters and to

> Exert your Soveraign Power, in Judgment sit . . . .
> Set forth your Edict, let it be enjoyn'd
> That all defective Species be recoyn'd . . . (p. 9).

By melting down and purifying the works of such offenders as Congreve, Southerne, Wycherley, and especially Dryden, and then coining new Wit England will be able to regain her balance. To administer the new coin Somers, Dorset, Sheffield, and Montague will establish a Bank of Wit, for

> These are good Men, in whom we all agree,
> Their Notes for Wit are good Security (p. 10).

Not many writers will meet the test of the new system. Even men like Vanbrugh and Congreve, who both "have Funds of Standard-Sense" will have to be careful, for "mix'd Metal oft they pass away"; similarly, Prior must give up his habit of descending to "facetious Fancies" (p. 11). Others less important—Codrington, Tate, etc.—will have to be improved, for there will be

> Small Places, for the little, loitt'ring Fry
> That follow G[ar]th or at Will Ur[win]'s ply.
> Their Station will be low, but ne'ertheless
> For this Provision they should Thanks express:
> 'Tis sad to be a Wit and Dinnerless (pp. 11-12).

Offenders against the new order will be branded. The principal criminals are those who

> Hold with *France* for Wit an Owling Trade (p. 13);

the worst of these is Garth:

> Felonious *G[arth]* pursuing this Design,
> Smuggles *French* Wit, as others Silks and Wine.[10]

Equally reprehensible are the writers who prostitute their profession by turning out panegyrics for wealthy fools, as Dryden did:

> D[ryde]n condemn who taught Men how to make
> Of Dunces Wits, an Angel of a Rake (p. 14).

All writers of satire should be suppressed, or at least let them

> . . . Be reform'd by cautious *D[or]set's* Test (p. 14),

for his satire is the result of " rich sense," while theirs flows "from want of Bread " (p. 14) :

> In *D[or]set* Wit (and therefore still 'twill please)
> Is Constitution, but in them Disease (p. 15).

Finally, a hospital should be set up for the weak and sick:

> And settle Doctors there of Worth and Skill.
> This Town can numbers for your Service spare,
> That live obscure and of Success despair . . . .
> And some such Doctors, sure you may persuade

---

[10] P. 13. Garth was accused of borrowing from Boileau's *Lutrin*, in his *Dispensary*. There is a marked similarity between Blackmore's lines, quoted above, and another writer's: " [The Fop Poet] is a Smuggler of Wit, and steals *French* Fancies without paying the customary Duties " (Judith Drake, *Essay in Defence of the Female Sex*, 1696, p. 79).

To labour at th' Appothecary's Trade.
They'll Med'cines make, and at the Mortar sweat,
Let 'em pound Drugs, they have no Brains to beat (p. 15).[11]

With the publication of the *Satyr against Wit* the tempo
of battle speeded up and Tom Brown's analysis of that poem
shows that already the Wits were marshalling their forces:

" A Friend of mine t'other Day, said a very pleasant thing,
methought upon this Occasion, a *Satyr against Wit*; that is,
says he, a *Satyr* against every endividual *Subject* King *William* has in his *Dominions*, for there's never a Man between
St. *Michael's Mount*, in *Cornwal*, and *Barwick upon Tweed*,
but thinks himself a *Wit*, whatever the World may think of
him; nay, I dare engage that our *Author* himself, for all his
Aversion to *Wit*, does not believe his *Satyr* to be without it.
'Tis the most fantastical Mixture of *Hypocrisie* and *Scandal*
you ever saw: The Writer of it sets up for an Advocate of

[11] In his " Essay upon Wit " (*Essays upon Several Subjects*, 1716) Blackmore gives a definition of Wit: " Wit is a Qualification of the Mind, that rises
and enlivens cold Sentiments and plain Propositions, by giving them an elegant
and surprizing Turn " (p. 191). While, then, in the *Satyr against Wit* Blackmore has nothing good to say of Wit, in the " Essay " he admits that Wit itself
is not of necessity evil; the harm lies rather in the base uses to which it is put
by its practitioners. It is usually allied with raillery, ridicule, satire, and vice,
and is by nature opposed to human understanding, reason, science, " instructive
and wise Discourse," " Justness and Propriety of Thoughts," and " Purity· of
Words and Expression " (pp. 190-192). It is commonly associated with levity
and dissolute manners and, what is more serious, frequently leads to the dis-
claiming of the Supreme Being (pp. 196-198). In the proper hands, however,
" Wit is that which imparts Spirit to our Conceptions and Diction, by giving
them a lively and novel, and therefore an agreeable Form . . . . Wit therefore
is the Accomplishment of a warm, sprightly, and fertile Imagination, enrich'd
with great Variety of proper Ideas . . . . The Addition of Wit to proper Subjects, is like the artful Improvement of the Cook, who by his exquisite Sauce
gives to a plain Dish, a pleasant and unusual Relish " (p. 192). Never can Wit
as a means of ornamentation be noble, for it can never rise above the " common
and less important Actions of Life."
    For additional information about Blackmore's ideas on Wit see my Intro-
duction to the Augustan Reprint Society's publication, Series One, No. 1 (May,
1946), pp. 1-5; Series One is devoted to pamphlets on Wit; No. 1 reprints Blackmore's *Essay upon Wit* and Addison's *Freeholder*, No. 45. See also Robert M.
Krapp, " Class Analysis of a Literary Controversy: Wit and Sense in Seventeenth Century English Literature," *Science and Society*, 10 (Winter, 1946),
82-83, 90-91.

Religion which he shews by his Scurrility, and want of good
Manners, and pretends that a *Confederacy* is carrying on in
Covent-Garden, to Banish *that* and *Learning* out of the
World. By the terrible Description he makes of some People,
one wou'd be apt to think that the *Goths* and *Vandals*, who
have been buried under Ground for so many hundred *Ages*,
were newly *sprung* up in *Russel-street*, and going with Fire
and Faggot in hand to set all our Libraries in Ashes; and
when that was done, to knock all the *Parsons* on the Head,
and ravish all the Women between *White-Hall* and *White-
Chapel*. But Dr. *Oates's* forty thousand *Pilgrims*, with their
Black Bills, and so forth, don't smell so rank of the *Legend*.
All the Reason I know he has to make this *hideous* Out-cry,
is, because the *Dispensary* has made bold to expose the
rumbling Fustian of his two *Arthurs*, and some honest Gentlemen, that now and then use to *drink* a *Dish* of *Tea* at
Will's, have been guilty of speaking the same truth. A strange
thing this! that a Man must be an *Atheist*, only for calling
Dullness by its proper Name, and a *Rake*, because he has
too much *Honesty* to Flatter one of the most execrable
Poems, that has plagu'd the World since the Days of *Quarles*
and *Ogilby*. As I told you before, the Author of this incomparable *Satyr* has been pleased to disown it; but he has
acknowledged enough to do his Business. He has own'd to a
Person of the *indelible* character, who complimented him
upon the Writing of it, and told him, that an *indelible* Mark
was stamped upon all his Works, that indeed he *Corrected*
and *Revised*, but did not *Write* it: Had any one but himself
been desired to *Correct* it, he wou'd have done it by whole-
sale with *Martial's Una litura*. However, this is enough in
all Conscience, for next to the Scandal of Writing such a confounded *Satyr*, that of Correcting and Revising it, deserves
the next place. But in *Satyr* and *Murder*, there's no such
thing as *Accessories*, but every Man is a *Principal*. It wou'd
look like too Solemn a Confutation of such *Ribaldry*, to say
that the *Gentlemen*, whom he has abused, have improved
and cultivated our Tongue, have obliged the World with
several Works that will be read with *Admiration*, and remembered with *Gratitude*, when his are forgotten; that they think
it no Disgrace to their *Learning*, to accompany it with *good
Manners*; that they know when to unbend themselves to
Pleasure, and when to apply to *Business*; that they don't

affect a *Gravity* which after all becomes none but *mysterious Block-heads*, nor show their *Morals*, by *censuring* those of their Neighbours: I say, it would look too *solemn*, to say any thing like this in their *Justification*, since not only their own *Works* speak for them, but they are sufficiently *commended*, by being made the *Heroes* of his Libel. Among other *merry* Doctrines he advances, he tells the World, that 'tis impossible for a Man to be a *Wit*, and not a *Rake*; this I suppose he calculated for the Meridian of *Cheapside*, and for the Consolation of his *City-Friends*, whom all the *World* will clear from the Imputation of being *Wits*: and yet, with all due Respect to my *Lord-Mayor* and *Aldermen* be it spoken, I believe there are as many of that Character within the *City-Walls*, as there are in *Covent-Garden*, and stupid senseless *Coxcombs* too, that discredit *Pleasure*, and Murder *that* which was design'd to enliven *Conversation*. He principally levels his Indignation at Mr. *Dryden*, and among other Sins, taxes him with *Flattery*. If Flattery is to be *Pardon'd* in any sort of Men, it certainly ought to be in the *Poets*; but for my part, I don't think them more *guilty* of it, than the *rest* of Mankind, who all *agree* to make their Court to *Wealth* and *Greatness*; and if it is a Sin to *flatter* Greatness, they do neither better nor worse than all the *World*, who, perhaps, have not the *same* Excuse. If a man were minded to be ill-natur'd, he might easily turn the *Tables* upon the *Church*, and show that the *Parsons* have *flatter'd* as much as the *Poets*. If the Latter in their Epistles Dedicatory bestow *Wit* and *Learning* upon *Block-heads*, the former have bestowed *Grace*, and the Lord knows how many *Christian Virtues* upon those that never possess'd them. What makes it look worse in the *Parsons* than the *Poets* is this, that these are privileged by their Function, whereas the former are Men of Grimace, and ought to abominate the least appearance of *Falsehood*, as much as they do *Non-payment* of Tithes. But 'tis a Jest, that the *City Bard* should fall foul upon any one for *Flattery*; he that has been guilty of the grossest, vilest *Flattery* imaginable, and prostituted the Dignity of an *Epic Poem*, more than any one before him. An *Epic Poem* is a noble magnificent Composition; the chief End of it is to excite Men to Virtue, by celebrating illustrious Examples, and proposing them to Imitation. 'Tis a Publick Building, like that of a *Temple*, or a *Town-Hall*; now as a

Man that designs to build any such *Structure*, if he intends
to *adorn* it with Statues, ought to set up those of *celebrated*
Men, of *Kings*, or *Princes*, or *Bishops*, and not his *Barber's*
because he Trims him well, or his *Shoemaker's*, because he
has got the Length of his Foot: So in an *Epic Poem*, an
Author should *only* introduce Men of *Figure* into his Work,
and not throw away his *Incense* upon *mean* or *obscure* Persons, merely because they are his *Friends*, and now and then
drink a Glass of Wine with him at the *Three Tuns* upon
Ludgate-Hill. Yet the Author of the Two *Arthurs*, has not
only done this, but has (to his Immortal Credit be it spoken)
introduced *Satyr* into an *Epic Poem*, which no one has done
before him, and I dare swear no one will ever attempt it after
him, except such a sordid Imitator, as he that has *Burlesqued*
our *Saviour* in *Heroick*. And Copies the *Faults* of all the
Authors he reads, instead of imitating their *Virtues*." [12]

The *Satyr* openly lays the blame for iniquitous Wit at the
feet of Dryden, Garth, Tom Brown, and others " debauch'd
by *D[ryde]n* and his Crew " (p. 12). It has been thought
until fairly recently that Dryden's wrath was aroused by
what are probably the most offensive lines in the whole
poem:

> Into the melting Pot when *D[ryde]n* comes,
> What horrid Stench will rise, what noisome Fumes?
> How will he shrink, when all his leud Allay,
> And wicked Mixture shall be purg'd away?
> When once his boasted Heaps are melted down,
> A Chest full scarce will yield one Sterling Crown (pp. 9-10),

even though Blackmore added:

> But what remains will be so pure, 'twill bear
> Th' Examination of the most severe.
> 'Twill S[ome]r's Scales and T[al]bot's Test abide,
> And with their Mark please all the World beside (p. 10).[13]

---

[12] " To Sir W. S——," in the *Works of . . . Voiture* (1705), 1701 section,
pp. 128-133.

[13] This passage has long held the attention of scholars. Sir Walter Scott confused the issue by stating that the last two couplets were intentionally omitted
by Blackmore after the first edition (*Works of Dryden*, ed. Scott-Saintsbury, I,

Macdonald, however, believes that it was not the passage quoted above but one in *Prince Arthur* that is responsible for Dryden's bitterness.[14] There, referring to Sakil's (Dorset's) patronage, Blackmore says:

> The Poets Nation, did Obsequious wait
> For the kind Dole, divided at his Gate.
> *Laurus* amidst the meagre Crowd appear'd,
> An old, revolted, unbelieving Bard,
> Who throng'd, and shov'd, and prest, and would be heard.
> Distinguish'd by his louder craving Tone,
> So well to all the Muses Patrons known,
> He did the Voice of modest Poets drown.
>
> (Bk. VI, p. 167)

But whatever the provocation was for Dryden's retorts, retort he did in several places. In 1700 Vanbrugh touched up Beaumont and Fletcher's *The Pilgrim* and presented it as a benefit for Dryden. Dryden himself furnished the Prologue, most of which he devoted to Blackmore:

> Quack Maurus, though he never took degrees
> In either of our universities,
> Yet to be shown by some kind wit he looks,
> Because he played the fool, and writ three books.
> But if he would be worth a poet's pen,
> He must be more a fool, and write again:
> For all the former fustian stuff he wrote
> Was dead-born, doggrel, or is quite forgot;
> His man of Uz, stript of his Hebrew robe,
> Is just the proverb, and "As poor as Job."
> One would have thought he could no longer jog;
> But Arthur was a level, Job's a bog.
> There though he crept, yet still he kept in sight;
> But here he founders in, and sinks downright.
> Had he prepared us, and been dull by rule,

---

354). Such, however, was not the case, though they were left out of the version in Blackmore's *Poems* (1718); see Hugh Macdonald, *John Dryden, a Bibliography* (Oxford, 1939), p. 291. No one has pointed out that the slur is apparently aimed at Dennis, Congreve, and Wycherley, as well as Dryden.

[14] *Ibid.*, pp. 282-283. See Macdonald's article, "The Attacks on Dryden," *Essays and Studies by Members of the English Association,* XXI (1936), 71-74.

Tobit had first been turned to ridicule;
But our bold Briton, without fear or awe,
O'erleaps at once the whole Apocrypha;
Invades the Psalms with rhymes, and leaves no room
For any Vandal Hopkins yet to come.
But when, if, after all, this godly gear
Is not so senseless as it would appear,
Our mountebank has laid a deeper train;
His cant, like Merry Andrew's noble vein,
Cat-calls the sects to draw them in again.
At leisure hours in Epic Song he deals,
Writes to the rumbling of his coach's wheels;
Prescribes in haste, and seldom kills by rule,
But rides triumphant between stool and stool.
Well, let him go, — 'tis yet too early day
To get himself a place in farce or play;
We know not by what name we should arraign him,
For no one category can contain him.
A pedant, canting preacher, and a quack,
Are load enough to break an ass's back.
At last, brown wanton, he presumed to write,
Traduced two kings, their kindness to requite;
One made the Doctor, and one dubbed the Knight.[15]

To his general dislike for Blackmore's poetry Dryden added, in the Preface to the *Fables* (1700), a more serious charge:

As for the City Bard, or Knight Physician, I hear his quarrel to me is, that I was the author of " Absalom and Achitophel," which, he thinks, is a little hard on his fanatic patrons in London. But I will deal the more civilly with his two poems, because nothing ill is to be spoken of the dead; and therefore, peace be to the manes of his " Arthurs." I will only say, that it was not for this noble knight that I drew the plan of an epic poem on King Arthur, in my preface to the translation of Juvenal. The guardian angels of kingdoms were machines too ponderous for him to manage; and therefore he rejected them, as Dares did the whirl-bats of Eryx, when they were thrown before him by Entellus: yet from that preface, he plainly took his hint; for he began immediately upon the

---

[15] *Works of Dryden*, ed. Scott-Saintsbury, VIII, 482-484. The Prologue was probably written between April 11 and 29 (H. Macdonald, *John Dryden, a Bibliography*, p. 135), not long before Dryden's death, on May 1.

story, though he had the baseness not to acknowledge his benefactory, but, instead of it, to traduce me in a libel.[16]

A close examination and comparison of Blackmore's epic with Dryden's plan reveal that the latter probably was justified in his claim of plagiarism.[17] Dryden gave Blackmore a final crack of the whip in his poem, " To My Honour'd Kinsman, John Driden," where he also praised Garth, one of the contributors to *Commendatory Verses*:

> . . . Maurus [Blackmore] sweeps whole parishes, and peoples
> every grave,
> And no more mercy to mankind will use,
> Than when he robbed and murdered Maro's muse.
> Would'st thou be soon dispatched, and perish whole,
> Trust Maurus with thy life, and M[i]lb[ou]rne with thy soul.[18]

It seems certain that Dryden's nerves were wearing thin. An old battle horse who had been in many a literary fray, Dryden, in his later days, found himself again under a cloud in Jeremy Collier's *Short View of the Immorality and Profaneness of the English Stage* (1698). Blackmore, who sided with Collier, was undoubtedly attacked by Dryden for his allegiance to such puritans as Collier, as well as for any particular lines he himself wrote. A lampoon well known at the time reads:

> John Dryden enemies had three,
> Sir Dick, Old Nick, and Jeremy:
> The doughty knight was forced to yield,
> The other two have kept the field.

---

[16] *Works of Dryden*, ed. Scott-Saintsbury, XI, 241-242. The "libel" mentioned at the end is, of course, the *Satyr against Wit*. It is sometimes thought that the *Satyr* appeared too late to be answered in the Preface to the *Fables*; see, for example, Johnson's *Lives of the Poets*, ed. G. B. Hill, I, 402, n. 2. However, Scott says that Luttrell's copy of the *Satyr* is dated November 23, 1699 (*Works of Dryden*, ed. Scott-Saintsbury, I, 352), well before Dryden's death.

[17] Roberta F. Brinkley, *Arthurian Legend in the Seventeenth Century* (Johns Hopkins Monographs in Literary History, Baltimore, 1932), p. 175. This book affords the most detailed analysis of Blackmore's Arthurian epics.

[18] *Works of Dryden*, ed. Scott-Saintsbury, XI, 76.

Neither faction emerged with flying colors, but probably Dryden's chief victory in his quarrel with Blackmore came in the publication of *Commendatory Verses*, shortly before he died. "Dryden and his crew" is a term one meets frequently in the *Commendatory Verses* squabble and most of the writers in that book (Tom Brown was one exception) were defenders of Dryden, the great god of Will's Coffee House. It is tempting to speculate on what his part in the collection was, for he must have been informed about its progress. At any rate, as far as Dryden is concerned, the reader who follows the Dryden-Blackmore quarrel from start to finish is inclined to agree with a contemporary writer of lampoons who suggests in an indecent piece that Blackmore's enemies would have been wiser to leave the City Bard alone.[19]

The storm center of the *Commendatory Verses* controversy was Will's Coffee House, which had begun to make its impression on literary London as early as 1660, Pepys reports.[20] It was not, however, until some years later that it became the throne room of Dryden, when "the appeal upon any literary dispute was made to him . . . . His armed chair, which in the winter had a settled and prescriptive place by the fire, was in the summer placed in the balcony . . . ."[21] After 1690 three separate clubs existed at Will's, which rapidly assumed the title of the "Wits' Coffee-house":

> At *Wills* you hear a Poem read,
> Where *Battus* from the Table-head,
> Reclining on his Elbow-chair,
> Gives Judgment with decisive Air.
> To whom the Tribe of circling Wits,
> As to an Oracle submits.[22]

There are many references in contemporary literature to the

[19] "*An* Epigram *upon Sir* R. B.," in Tom Brown, *Works* (1715), I, 77.
[20] *The Diary of Samuel Pepys* (1924), ed. H. B. Wheatley, I, 16-17.
[21] Johnson, *Lives of the Poets*, ed. G. B. Hill, I, 408-409.
[22] "On Poetry: a Rapsody," in *The Poems of Jonathan Swift*, ed. H. Williams (Oxford, 1937), II, 649.

drunken Julian, peddler of lampoons, the most famous of which is Dryden's "Familiar Epistle to Mr. Julian, Secretary of the Muses," [23] and the proprietor, Will Urwin, who died in 1695. The death of Dryden in 1700 marked the end of the halcyon days at Will's, as Steele points out in the first number of the *Tatler*: "This place is very much altered since Mr. Dryden frequented it; where you used to see songs, epigrams, and satires in the hands of every man you met, you now have only a pack of cards; and instead of cavils about the turn of the expression, the elegance of the style, and the like, the learned now dispute only about the truth of the game." [24] *Commendatory Verses* was a product of the declining years of Will's:

. . . When the *Cheapside* Poet, at the Expence of proclaiming himself a Fool, publish'd a Satyr against *Wit*, What Tumults, what Storms did he raise? All *Will's* was presently in Arms; both Commission'd and Non-commission'd Officers rais'd Forces against the common Enemy; raw, unexperienced Soldiers, nay, Women were Listed to make up a compleat Army; Men of the Sword, Physicians, Lawyers, young Students, Punsters, Topers, ingenious Ladies, *Drury-lane* Poetesses; in a word, all the *Wits* and *Witlings* thought themselves engag'd in Honour to revenge the Affront; and Headed by a fierce Leader, with *Pointed* or *Blunt* Epigrams, no matter which, march'd out in Battle-Array, to fight their bold Antagonist.[25]

Jeremy Collier's *Short View* concerns us here because of the kinship of purpose that existed between Blackmore and Collier and also because the attack hit many of the Wits at Will's who later participated in the writing of *Commendatory Verses*. It is usually agreed that Collier had a case, for the notorious Restoration drama had frequently gone beyond the bounds of conventional moral decorum. Once again John

---

[23] *Works of Dryden*, ed. Scott-Saintsbury, XV, 217-219. See Brice Harris, "Robert Julian, Secretary to the Muses," *ELH*, 10 (1943), 294-309.

[24] See Robert J. Allen, *The Clubs of Augustan London* (Harvard Studies in English, VII; Cambridge, Mass., 1933), pp. 27-32.

[25] "Mr. B—— to Mr. C——," August 10, 1700, in *Letters of Wit, Politicks, and Morality*, ed. Abel Boyer, 1701, pp. 250-251.

Dennis was designated as defender of the Wits, though once again he probably did not go as far as they wished in answering the opposition. Dennis's *Usefulness of the Stage, to the Happiness of Mankind, to Government, and to Religion, Occasioned by a Late Book, Written by Jeremy Collier, M.A.* (1698) was the first comprehensive reply to the reformer. Dennis takes a moderate view of Collier's charge of immorality on the stage. He doesn't object, he says, to Collier's attacking the licentiousness of the drama—in fact, he is sympathetic to such a crusade—but he does object to Collier's labeling all drama as evil.[26] While Collier himself comes in for less abuse in *Commendatory Verses* than might be expected, Blackmore is definitely linked with the Collier campaign. He is told:

> You weakly Skirmish with the Sins o' th' Age,
> And are the errant Scavinger o' th' Stage.[27]

Dr. Johnson compares the part played by the two reformers: ". . . Blackmore's censure was cold and general, Collier's was personal and ardent: Blackmore taught his reader to dislike what Collier incited him to abhor." [28]

The wrangling which resulted in the publication of *Commendatory Verses* is made still more complex by the intrusion of bickering in medical circles over the establishment of a dispensary. The apothecaries and doctors had carried on open warfare for years. The former, frequently uneducated dabblers (even grocers were allowed to dispense drugs), not merely content with dealing in drugs, were even permitted by law to practice phlebotomy. In 1617, however, the apothecaries were put under the control of the College of Physicians, a move which resulted in much bitter feeling, partly because the doctors in some instances were not much better prepared to dispense drugs than were the apothecaries. The apothe-

---

[26] *Dennis*, ed. Hooker, I, 146-147.
[27] " Friendly Advice to Dr. Bl———," in *Commendatory Verses*, p. 17.
[28] *Lives of the Poets*, II, 241.

caries promptly registered a protest by ignoring the law; they could also, by boycotting a doctor and refusing him drugs, ruin him. Then, too, a doctor's care usually came high, and there were many who could not afford this luxury. In 1688 the College of Physicians, recognizing the difficulty, drew up plans for a laboratory of their own which would prepare medicines for charity cases. Charging that the doctors were really interested in a dispensary only as a money-making scheme, the apothecaries succeeded in splitting the ranks of the College itself. Enforced coöperation with the dispensary failed, and the proponents of the plan were driven to collecting subscriptions, and in this way were able for a while to sell drugs at cost. Having a social, as well as a medical, purpose, the dispensary soon drew the attention of the whole country, particularly Grub Street. Sir Samuel Garth brought the matter to a head by publishing, in 1699, his *Dispensary,* which is frequently given the credit for bringing popular approval to the project. Even Dryden entered the lists and defended Garth in his " To My Honour'd Kinsman, John Driden." [29]

In his mock-heroic poem Garth has Blackmore quote some of his own verses, to which a Fury replies:

> Mortal, how dar'st thou with such Lines Address
> My awful Seat, and trouble my Recess . . . ?
> Then dare not, for the future, once rehearse
> The Dissonance of such unequal Verse.
> But in your Lines let Energy be found,
> And learn to rise in Sense, and sink in Sound.
> Harsh words, tho' pertinent, uncouth appear,
> None please the Fancy, who offend the Ear.
> In Sense and Numbers if you wou'd excel,
> Read W[ycherle]y, consider D[ry]den well . . .
> Such just Examples carefully read o'er,
> Slide without falling, without straining soar.

---

[29] This account is based on Dr. Harvey Cushing's " Dr. Garth: The Kit-Cat Poet," in the *Bulletin of the Johns Hopkins Hospital,* 17, No. 178 (January, 1906), 2-4.

Oft tho' your Stroaks surprise, you shou'd not choose,
A Theme so mighty for a Virgin Muse.
Long did *Appelles* his Fam'd Piece decline,
His *Alexander* was his last Design.
'Tis *M[onta]gue's* rich Vein alone must prove.
None but a *Phidias* shou'd attempt a *Jove.*[30]

Garth also contributed some lines to *Commendatory Verses*
attacking Blackmore; *Commendatory Verses* is, in fact, full
of the Dispensary quarrel. Tom Brown, the editor of *Commendatory Verses,* may have already taken sides in the play
Physick Lies A-Bleeding (1697) ;[31] Christopher Codrington
and Charles Boyle, who played an important part in the
publication of the miscellany, had written laudatory poems
to Garth which were prefixed to the *Dispensary.* On the other
side, Blackmore had shown his scorn of the *Dispensary* in
the closing lines of the *Satyr against Wit. Discommendatory
Verses,* too, devotes a considerable amount of attention to
defending such anti-Dispensarians as Gibbons and Ratcliffe
and running down Drake and Colbatch, members of Garth's
camp.

One other tangential literary quarrel plays an important
part in *Commendatory Verses* and *Discommendatory Verses,*
the question of the authenticity of the epistles of Phalaris.[32]
Sir William Temple began the argument in his essay, *On
Ancient and Modern Learning* (1690), by taking the stand
that the ancients surpassed the moderns in literature, science,
and the arts, and offering as evidence of this superiority the
excellence of the *Epistles of Phalaris.* He was answered in

[30] Third Edition, 1699, pp. 55-57.

[31] *Physick lies a Bleeding, or the Apothecary turned Doctor. A Comedy,
Acted every Day in most Apothecaries Shops in London* (1697). Although Tom
Brown was announced as the author he denied the authorship. Professor Benjamin Boyce suggests that the ruse may have been an attempt to stir up trouble
between Brown and his wealthy patron, Dr. Baynard (*Tom Brown of Facetious
Memory* [Cambridge, Mass.], 1939, pp. 59-60). However, Brown did edit the
pro-Dispensary *Commendatory Verses* only three years later; Baynard himself
may have had a hand in *Commendatory Verses* (see below, p. 134).

[32] The best and most detailed analysis of the matter is to be found in R. C.
Jebb's *Bentley* (English Men of Letters, New York, 1882), pp. 39-94.

1694 by William Wotton, a friend of the classical scholar, Richard Bentley, in his *Reflections on Ancient and Modern Learning*. The Wits entered the argument by having their representative, Charles Boyle, put out a new edition of the *Epistles*; he took occasion in his Preface to make insulting remarks about Bentley, the giant of the opposition. To the second edition of Wotton's *Reflections* (1697) Bentley contributed an essay on the epistles showing that they were not written in 600 B.C., as Temple had claimed, but were forgeries of the early Christian era. Boyle and the Wits again replied, and fashionable literary London agreed that the musty scholar had been put to flight. However, in March of 1699 Bentley's *Dissertation on the Letters of Phalaris* appeared. This book, one of the great contributions to English classical scholarship, made use of Bentley's knowledge of philology and a scientific method in general to help introduce a new kind of criticism. At the turn of the eighteenth century, however, Bentley's victory was less certain than it is today. Tom Brown's unfavorable comments are typical of those circulating among the coffee houses:

You and I, and every Body has been charm'd with the Honourable Mr. *Boyle's* Answer to a stiff haughty *Grammarian* that shall be nameless, but is known well enough. Never did Wit and Learning Triumph so gloriously over Dullness and Pedantry, as in that noble Book; and never was any Argument managed with that Variety of Learning, and those agreeable *Turns* of *Wit*. Accordingly it found a kind Reception not only in *England*, but *abroad*. The *Foreign Journals*, gave it the Commendation it deserved, and all the *Polite Judges* in *Europe* were pleased to see an *Arrogant Pedant*, that had been crouding his Head twenty Years together with the Spoils of *Lexicons* and *Dictionaries*, worsted and foiled by a *Young Gentleman*, upon his own *Dunghil*, and by his own *Criticisms*. Thus one would have thought that Mr. *Boyle's* Merit and Quality would have *secured* him from any *scurrilous* Treatment; and that his *Enemies*, if he could have any such, wou'd be content to *Envy* him in Private, and never have the Impudence to *Attack* him in Publick.[33]

---

[33] "To Sir W. S——," in the *Works of* . . . *Voiture* (1701 section), pp. 133-134.

Commendatory Verses reflects in many places the Wits' scorn for Bentley and their admiration for Boyle; a reading of the pages of *Commendatory Verses* alone would convince the reader that Boyle had indeed triumphed. To the Wits, dictating literary tastes from Will's, the impressive learning of Bentley's work meant little; rather, they were swayed by Boyle's style of writing, which they found superior to Bentley's. Swift's attack on that scholar in Section 3 of the *Tale of a Tub* represents this popular attitude, which paved the way for a fourth edition of Boyle's reply as late as 1744; and in 1749 Thomas Francklin, who later became Regius Professor of Greek, published a translation of the Phalaris epistles and still claimed that they were genuine. Even Cumberland, Bentley's grandson, was apologizing for the great scholar's conclusions as late as 1804.[34] Apparently Bentley was singled out for attack in *Commendatory Verses* (next to Blackmore himself he is jeered at more than anyone else) because he had the temerity to challenge Boyle, one of the darlings of Will's. This special attention to Bentley is underlined by the fact that most of the slurring remarks about him are made by Codrington, Boyle's great friend and probably the leader in the publication of *Commendatory Verses*.

Certainly posterity does not back up the Wits in their low opinion of Bentley, who is looked on today as one of the greatest of English classical scholars.[35] On the other hand,

[34] R. C. Jebb, *Bentley*, pp. 75-76, 79-80.

[35] The traditional adoration of Bentley is expressed in the following passage: "[*Phalaris*] established his reputation as the first critic of the age among discerning readers at home and among leading scholars abroad. Even now, after more than two centuries, when our knowledge of many phases of classical antiquity is vastly greater than in Bentley's day, the consummate mastery of his exposition, like the astonishing range of his knowledge, embracing with equal ease Greek and Latin authors, religion, social customs, numismatics, metrology, and other branches of archaeology, fills one with awe; while the vigorous style, slightly colloquial, now witty, now shot through with biting sarcasm, carries the reader along breathlessly even through the discussion of scholarly *minutiae* which in other hands would, however learned, have become insufferably arid

Boyle's part too has in modern times commonly been mis-judged, for he is usually condemned as a fool. Jebb reminds us that Boyle, contrary to what is usually thought, never did maintain that the epistles were genuine. In fact, he him-self had expressed doubt as to their authenticity. But he did deny that Bentley had proved them spurious.[36] Nor was Bentley's distinction that of merely advancing the theory that the epistles were fakes, for others before him had already suggested it. His task was rather to give proof to support such an assertion.[37] Bentley crushed his opponents by sheer weight of scholarship and learning, giving impetus to one of the great literary quarrels of the eighteenth century, that over the relative merits of the ancients and the moderns. Swift's attack on Bentley in *The Battle of the Books* (1704), the peak of the controversy, was inspired by a desire to defend his former patron, and by a dislike of what he called pedantry in Bentley and Wotton.[38]

* * * * *

Upon examining the causes contributing to the issues in *Commendatory Verses* after two and a half centuries, we find that the matter is still clouded. Certainly most scholars today would side with Bentley against Charles Boyle and his " witty " friends; some would support Collier (thus indi-rectly lending weight to Blackmore's cause); practically all

---

and dull " (M. L. W. Laistner, "Richard Bentley: 1742-1942," *SP*, 39 [1942], 512). At least one classical scholar, however, has raised a dissenting voice. In discussing Bentley's work on Horace, B. L. Ullman sets forth his objections to this hero worship. Bentley was, he says, (1) lacking in a sense of humor; (2) deficient in poetic feeling and applied " the searing blast of inexorable logic to the poet's fragile flowers "; (3) without an understanding of figures of speech; (4) too strict in his syntax. The harm in this greatly overrated scholar, Ullman maintains, is that he has wrongly inspired an awe which has kept others from questioning his work and his greatness (" Horace and the Philologians," *Classical Journal*, 31 [1935], 407-409).

[36] R. C. Jebb, *Bentley*, p. 55.

[37] *Ibid.*, pp. 72-73.

[38] Ricardo Quintana, *The Mind and Art of Jonathan Swift* (Oxford, 1936), p. 76.

would be in favor of the humanitarian aims of the Dispensary. Objectivity, particularly when it has not been sharpened by historical perspective, is seldom strong at the time of actual conflict, and so we find writers at the turn of the eighteenth century lined up belligerently (for the most part) either for Blackmore or against him. Some anti-Blackmoreans added their voices to the hue and cry raised by the Wits. One of these, Judith Drake, leaves no doubt as to her opinion: "I honour the Names, and admire the Writings of *Denham, Suckling,* and *D'avenant,* I am ravish'd with the Fancy of *Cowley,* and the Gallantry of *Waller.* I reverence the *Fairy Queen,* am rais'd, and elevated with *Paradise Lost, Prince Arthur* composes and reduces me to a State of Yawning indifference . . . ."[39]   Another Lady, Mrs. Elizabeth Thomas, writing shortly after the publication of Dryden's *Fables* (1700), in the Preface to which Blackmore is attacked, affects great scorn for Blackmore and states her preference for Garth and his *Dispensary.*[40]   John Oldmixon greeted Blackmore's success with *Prince Arthur* with a bitter comment:

> Still in this wretched Trade I pass my days.
> So low, that *B*—— can my Envy raise,
> Oh! happy *B*—— thy prodigious Muse,
> Huge Books of Verse can in a year produce.
> True—— Rude and Dull, to some she gives offence,
> And seems Created in despite of sense;
> Yet she will find whatever we have said,
> Both Sots to Print her Works, and Fools to read.[41]

Another writer, turning Blackmore's own figure of melted-down Wit against him, says:

. . . As to *Heroick Poetry,* methinks he Reasons thus with himself; Homer has writ the *Ilias* and the *Odysseis,* and *Virgil* only the *Aeneid;*

---

[39] *Essay in Defence of the Female Sex* (1696), p. 50.

[40] *Pylades and Corinna* (Second Edition, 1736), II, 179.

[41] "The Second Satire of Boileau, English'd," in *Poems on Several Occasions* (1696), pp. 72-73.

I have writ *Prince Arthur* and *King Arthur*; am I not then equal to *Homer*, and Superior to *Virgil*? No, B——re, we judge of *Poetry* as we do of *Metals*, not by the *Lump*, but the intrinsick Value. New-cast your Poems, purge 'em to the Bulk of the *Dispensary*, and if then they weigh in the Balance with *that*, we will allow you a Place among the First-rate *Heroick Poets*.[42]

Although at this point a summing up of the evidence seems to give the advantage to the Wits, who in *Commendatory Verses*

> . . . Take a World of Pains,
> To shew that both the *Arthurs* had no Brains;
> And labour hard to bring Authentick Proof,
> That he that wrote Wit's Satyr was an Oaf,[43]

we should not forget that Blackmore had his supporters, some of whom, such as Defoe and Locke, were not inconsiderable. The *Epistle to Sr. Richard Blackmore* (1700) stated to Blackmore that the Wits

> . . . All in Council do together sit
> How to dethrone the beamy God of Wit;
> How to defame all virtuous Men that write,
> They rally Forces, and their Strength unite.
> This, Sir's your Fate, curs'd *Criticks* you oppose,
> The most Tyrannical and cruel Foes:
> Dr[yde]n their Huntsman dead, he no more wounds,
> But now you must engage his Pack of Hounds . . . .
> To move their Rubbish you yourself demean,
> Yet cannot this *Augean Stable* clean;
> The nest of Viper-Criticks there you found,
> Their snaky Heads erect, and hissing round . . . .

In dedicating his *Triumph of Peace, a Poem* (1698) to Blackmore, John Hughes maintained that that writer "has given the World a noble Instance that good Morals and good Poetry are very consistent." Edward Howard put Blackmore

---

[42] *The English Theophrastus: or, The Manners of the Age* (1702), p. 2. This collection is made up of extracts from other, unidentified, writers.
[43] *A New Session of the Poets* (1700), p. 2.

on an equal footing with Milton,[44] an opinion echoed by
William Molyneux, who wrote to John Locke:

> I perceive you are so happy as to be acquainted with sir Richard
> Blackmore: he is an extraordinary person, and I admire his two prefaces
> as much as I do any parts of his books: the first, wherein he exposed
> the " licentiousness and immorality of our late poetry," is incomparable;
> and the second, wherein he prosecutes the same subject and delivers his
> thoughts concerning hypothesis, is no less judicious . . . . Mr. Churchill
> favoured me with the present of sir R. Blackmore's K. Arthur. I had
> Pr. Arthur before, and read it with admiration, which is not at all les-
> sened by this second piece. All our English poets (except Milton) have
> been mere ballad-makers in comparison to him.[45]

Locke himself wrote to Molyneux: ". . . Sir R. B.'s vein in
poetry be what every body must allow him to have an
extraordinary talent in . . . . The Preface to *King Arthur*
shows as great a strength and penetration of judgment, as
his poetry has showed flights of fancy . . . .[46] That Blackmore had a substantial reading public is seen in the fact that
Prince Arthur went through three editions in rapid succes-
sion, was translated into Latin by W. Hogg in 1700, and
came out in duodecimo in 1714. This popularity is also reflected in the contemporary marginal comment in a Harvard
copy: "Let them say what they please, damn them, this is
a great epick poem."[47] In other words, though unfortunately
for Blackmore his admirers did less about putting their sentiments into print than did his opponents, there can be little
doubt that Blackmore's *Satyr against Wit*, published late in
November of 1699, the immediate cause of *Commendatory
Verses*, was well received in many quarters. Blackmore, along
with Collier, was fast assuming the rôle of a self-appointed

---

[44] *Essay on Pastoral, and Elegy on Queen Mary, Proem* (1695), as quoted
in *The Library of Literary Criticism*, ed. C. W. Moulton (Buffalo, 1901), II, 746.

[45] Molyneux to Locke, in Locke's *Works* (1823), July 20, 1695, IX, 429;
May 27, 1697, IX, 423.

[46] Sept. 11, 1697, *ibid.*, IX, 432-433.

[47] Quoted by Howard Maynadier, in *The Arthur of the English Poets* (Boston
and New York, 1907), p. 302.

Moses who would lead the age out of the morass of moral degradation. In the Preface to his *Job* (1700) he says:

> If I can escape the Defamation of their [Wits] Panegyricks, I think myself very safe. I have no Personal Quarrel with any of the *Writers* I have censur'd; and if they think fit to *expose* my Name for asserting the *Cause* of *Vertue* and *Religion*, I have no reason to be displeased with them for doing me so *great* an *Honour* (p. iii).

II. BLACKMORE'S LATER REPUTATION

A S FAR AS the Wits of *Commendatory Verses* were concerned, the Knight of Cheapside was a fool, a quack,
a sham, and an unspeakably bad poet, a picture which posterity has done little to soften. No doubt Blackmore's unfortunate skill at antagonizing such merciless satirists as Pope
and Swift has had much to do with his harsh treatment and
the perpetuation of the portrait first set up in *Commendatory Verses*. Blackmore's initial skirmish with Pope did not
take place until 1717, when he attacked *Three Hours after
Marriage* and *A Roman Catholick Version of the First
Psalm*:

> I cannot but here take notice, that one of these Champions of Vice
> is the reputed Author of a detestable Paper, that has lately been handed
> about in Manuscript, and now appears in Print, in which the godless
> Author has burlesqu'd the *First Psalm of David* in so obscene and pro-
> fane a manner, that perhaps no Age ever saw such an insolent affront
> offer'd to the establish'd Religion of their Country, and this, good
> Heaven! with Impunity. A sad Demonstration this, of the low Ebb to
> which the *British* Vertue is reduc'd in these degenerate Times.[1]

This statement, together with the fact that Blackmore
was one of Curll's authors, was enough to win the City Bard
a doubtful immortality in the *Dunciad*:

[1] From *Essays upon Several Subjects*, II (1717), as quoted in Pope's *Imita-
tions of Horace*, Twickenham Edition, ed. John Butt, IV (London, 1939), 346.
Norman Ault maintains that Pope's burlesque has been misunderstood; that it
was not meant to be a parody of the *First Psalm*, but only a " mockery of
Sternhold's pedestrian verses "; that it was not intended for publication, but
was written solely for the amusement of coffee-house patrons (" New Light on
Pope," *RES*, 28 (1934), 441-447, especially 445-446).

> But far o'er all, sonorous Blackmore's strain;
> Walls, steeples, skies, bray back to him again.
> In Tot'nam fields, the brethren, with amaze,
> Prick all their ears up, and forget to graze;
> Long Chanc'ry-lane retentive rolls the sound,
> And courts to courts return it round and round;
> Thames wafts it thence to Rufus' roaring hall,
> And Hungerford re-echoes bawl for bawl.
> All hail him victor in both gifts of song,
> Who sings so loudly, and who sings so long.[2]

With equally bad judgment Blackmore attacked Swift's
Tale of a Tub, in the " Essay upon Wit ":

Had this Writing been publish'd in a Pagan or Popish Nation, who
are justly impatient of all Indignity Offer'd to the Establish'd Religion
of their Country, no doubt but the Author would have receiv'd the
Punishment he deserv'd. But the Fate of this impious Buffoon is very
different; for in a Protestant Kingdom, zealous of their Civil and Religious Immunities, he has not only escap'd Affronts and the Effects of
publick Resentment, but has been caress'd and patroniz'd by Persons of
great Figure and of all Denominations.[3]

Gay rushed to Swift's defence in his poem, " Verses to be
placed under the Picture of England's Arch Poet ":

> [Blackmore] maul'd human wit in one thick satire,
> Next, in three books, sunk human nature;
> Undid creation at a jerk,
> And of redemption made damn'd work.[4]

But as the City Knight advanced in life his critics directed
their lampoons at his poetry, although his medical preten-
sions and his knighthood were always good for a jibe. The

---

[2] Twickenham Edition, ed. James Sutherland (London, 1943), 308.

[3] *Essays upon Several Subjects* (1716), p. 217.

[4] *Poems of John Gay* (Muses Library, London, n.d., ed. J. Underhill), II,
255. It has been suggested that this poem may not be by Gay; it is sometimes
attributed to Swift and even to Arbuthnot (*Poetical Works of John Gay*, ed.
G. C. Faber [London, 1926], p. xxv). However, see George Sherburn, *The Early
Career of Alexander Pope* (Oxford, 1934), p. 167, n. 4. Blackmore's *Creation*
appeared in 1712; his *Redemption*, in 1722.

epics, quite properly, came in for the worst drubbing, for besides exhibiting some atrocious passages, they offended by their sheer mass and dreariness.

Had Blackmore been a mere versifier he might have escaped with little more punishment than being shunted into the limbo of mediocrity. Fortunately for Blackmore, however, it was his lot by an accident of history to play a small part as a promoter of the bourgeois morality which in the eighteenth century became increasingly important. After 1700 Blackmore, while continuing to draw on English legend and history for his *Eliza* (1705) and *Alfred* (1723), began to beat a new path for himself in religious subjects, particularly in *Job* (1700) and *Creation* (1712). Thus did he take a further step in the direction indicated in his early works and solidly set himself up as a champion of Christianity. For those who had supported Collier and Blackmore in their attack on the immorality of the stage and their castigation of the Wits, this move was not a surprise. Few even of his friends defended the poetic quality of the early epics, but here they had a persecuted Galahad they could rally around, a poet with a strong fervor for religion. With the publication of *Creation* Blackmore became firmly entrenched and by 1720 was no longer considered a fool by all. Even some of his old enemies did an about-face; [5] Steele praised him in the *Spectator*, No. 6, and John Dennis said that *Creation* surpassed Lucretius.[6] Addison, about whom Blackmore had made slurring remarks in the *Satyr against Wit*, obliged with a compliment in the *Spectator*, No. 339:

> [*The Creation*] deserves to be looked upon as one of the most useful and noble productions in our English verse. The reader cannot but be pleased to find the depths of philosophy enlivened with all the charms of poetry, and to see so great a strength of reason, amidst so beautiful a redundancy of the imagination.

---

[5] According to one story, the Wits themselves had a hand in polishing up *Creation* (Johnson, *Lives of the Poets*, II, 243).

[6] "Remarks upon Mr. Pope's Translation of Homer " (1717), in *Dennis*, ed. Hooker, II, 107, 120.

The modern scholar is likely to lose sight of this side of Blackmore's reputation, for the accepted judgment is that the Wits, in *Commendatory Verses* especially, put Blackmore to flight for all time. However, Watts' praises in the Preface to the *Horae Lyricae*, Locke's and Molyneux's approbation, and Addison's remarks about *Creation* show that even in his own day Blackmore had a small but ardent group of followers.[7] This sympathy points out once again the error of regarding the views of the fashionable poets as the only opinions of the times, of looking on the works of Dryden and the other "Restoration" writers as the only literary creations the age produced. While Blackmore's supporters were never so vocal as the opposition, they represented, as the following judgment by a mid-eighteenth century biographer demonstrates, a puritan spirit which is always present in literature in some degree:

He was a chaste writer; he struggled in the cause of virtue, even in those times, when vice had the countenance of the great, and when an almost universal degeneracy prevailed. He was not afraid to appear the advocate of virtue, in opposition to the highest authority, and no lustre of abilities in his opponents could deter him from stripping vice of those gaudy colours, with which poets of the first eminence had cloathed her.[8]

To the last, Sir Richard Blackmore remained the champion of virtue and the enemy of what he considered to be literary wickedness; he continued the fight even after death:

[7] The fame of this Heavy Poet, however problematical elsewhere, was universally received in the City of London " (*The Works of Alexander Pope Esq.*, ed. William Warburton, 1752, IV, 102). Instances of Blackmore's defense through the period of the *Commendatory Verses* quarrel are given above (see pp. 26-28); his admirers continued to point out his virtues. William Coward praised *Prince Arthur* for showing the elegancies of the English tongue (*Licentia Poetica Discuss'd, or the True Test of Poetry*, 1709, p. 23), while Thomas Foxton, in *The Character of a Fine Gentleman* . . . (1721, p. 59), says that his perfect (and pious) gentleman, Serino, was fondest of Milton, and after Milton Blackmore's *Creation*, Watts' *Horae Lyricae*, and Young's poem on the Last Day.

[8] Robert Shiels and Theophilus Cibber, *Lives of the Poets of Great Britain and Ireland, to the Time of Dean Swift* (1753), V, 178.

If Richard Blackmore Hurst die before the age of 21, then £1000 to Oxford University to the Vice Chancellors and other Heads of Houses, to elect a student or Member of the University to write poems on divine subjects six months in every year, giving preference to St. Edmund's hall, viz:— 650 lines in verse to be approved by the Vice chancellor & for the other six months to write some discourse in prose to censure & discourage all profane obscene plays, poems, & other immoral writings which shall be published alternately each half year; each student elected to continue for 7 years.[9]

The purely religious appeal of Blackmore's works is perhaps best seen in American literature. For Cotton Mather, Blackmore was "the incomparable" poet whose lines are scattered throughout the writings of that Colonial divine.[10] Another New England minister, Benjamin Colman, taught his daughter to regard Blackmore as next "after the Reverend Doctor Watts," the true "laureate of the Church of Christ."[11] Nor should we forget that Blackmore shared with Pope the distinction of having the greatest influence on early eighteenth-century American poetry in general.[12] In England John Wesley was in the van of Blackmore's defenders and, as the leader of a middle class religion, demonstrated the strong faith of that class in Blackmore.[13] In general, as might be expected, they liked Blackmore on religious, not poetic, grounds, for they were "that numerous and sober class of readers, who think that genius consists in good intention."[14]

That this touting of Blackmore as a Christian hero was not lacking in effectiveness is best seen in Dr. Johnson's

[9] Blackmore's will is given in E. Hudson Long, "Notes on Sir Richard Blackmore," *MLN*, 58 (1943), 589.

[10] See, for instance, *The Christian Philosopher* (1721), p. 211.

[11] E. Turell, *Memoirs of Mrs. Jane Turell* (1741), pp. 29-30, as quoted in Moses C. Tyler, *History of American Literature* (New York, 1879), II, 44.

[12] William P. Trent, *History of American Literature, 1607-1865* (New York, 1920), p. 82.

[13] As one example of this esteem it might be noted that the *Collection of Divine Hymns and Poems upon Several Occasions* (Third Edition, 1719) was dedicated to Blackmore.

[14] Sir Walter Scott, *Works of John Dryden*, I, 437.

reaffirmation of Blackmore's stand eighty years after the
publication of *Commendatory Verses*. Johnson's intention
of doing a life of Blackmore was hailed by Mrs. Thrale:

> Blackmore . . . will be rescued from the old wits who worried him,
> much to your disliking; so a little for love of his Christianity, a little for
> love of his physick, a little for love of his courage and a little for love
> of contradiction, you will save him from the malevolent criticks, and
> perhaps do him the honour to devour him yourself.[15]

At Johnson's insistence Blackmore was added to his edition
of the English poets, though he was careful to print *Creation*
as the only example of his poetic skill. Too shrewd a critic
in spite of himself to give blanket approval to all of Blackmore's works—he did, in fact, censure some of them—Johnson, like most defenders of the City Knight, placed the
emphasis on his plea for morality:

> Blackmore, by the unremitted enmity of the wits, whom he pro-
> voked more by his virtue than his dulness, has been exposed to worse
> treatment than he deserved; his name was so long used to point every
> epigram upon dull writers that it became at last a bye-word of con-
> tempt . . . . While the distributors of literary fame were endeavouring
> to depreciate and degrade him he either despised or defied them, wrote
> on as he had written before, and never turned aside to quiet them by
> civility or repress them by confutation.[16]

In his prose essays also, we are told, Blackmore "took little
care to propitiate the wits, for he scorned to avert their
malice at the expence of virtue or of truth." [17] The reader
of the often scurrilous *Discommendatory Verses*, however,
will find it hard to believe that Blackmore "seems to have
been more delighted with praise than pained by censure," [18]
though he may agree with Boswell that the City Knight,
like Dr. Johnson, "*enjoyed* the perpetual shower of little

---

[15] Mrs. Thrale to Dr. Johnson, May 9, 1780, *Piozzi Letters*, II, 122, as
quoted in Boswell's *Life of Johnson*, ed. Powell-Hill, IV, 55, n. 1.

[16] *Lives of the Poets*, ed. G. B. Hill, II, 252-253.

[17] *Ibid.*, p. 247.   [18] *Ibid.*, p. 239.

hostile arrows." [19] It is doubtful if Johnson's attempt to reclaim Blackmore's reputation added anything new to the criticism of that writer.[20] But since popular anthologies and histories of literature of the late eighteenth and nineteenth centuries quoted Dr. Johnson on Blackmore extensively, it is safe to assume that he did much to keep alive a small but steady flame of interest in a minor poet who would otherwise have been forgotten.

In our day Blackmore has slipped quietly into near oblivion. His poems are no longer reprinted, even in part, and his name is kept alive only by scholars interested in his relation to Dryden, Swift, Pope, or the epic; thus Blackmore has achieved what Saintsbury calls "an uncomfortable immortality." [21] The clan of worshipers has few modern descendants, for those who by temperament might be expected to defend Blackmore have turned their attention elsewhere, possibly to such contemporary writers as Lloyd Douglas. The few staunch souls who read Blackmore today are as venomous in their comments as were Tom Brown and Christopher Codrington. One writer says of the epics of Blackmore, Glover, and Wilkie: "We now enter the most desolate region of English poetry, a dreary 'No Man's Land,' forbidding desert, without sign of human occupation or interest, a region reported to be barren beyond hope, shunned even by the most hardy seekers for poetic treasure, through which few, if any, living travellers have ever forced their way . . ."; another confesses: "I have not read all of his verse, but my bibliography will show that I have suffered

[19] *Life of Johnson*, ed. Powell-Hill, IV, 55.

[20] That the opposition was still alive is seen from the following comment by James Beattie, written about the same time as Johnson's remarks given above: "The poet seems to have had no notion of any thing more magnificent, than the usages of his own time and neighborhood; which, accordingly, he transfers to the most awful subjects, and thus degrades what he meant to raise to sublimity " (*Essays*, 1779, p. 357).

[21] *CHEL*, IX, 177.

enough." [22] The kindest judgments are those which partially excuse Blackmore on the far from complimentary grounds that he was not intentionally dull. While a few creditable passages can be found in his works, these critics say, his chief offense is his lack of taste. " He was a commonplace man with an amiable faith in himself, and without intellect to distinguish between good and bad in poetry," [23] is a typical summing up. Certainly, as Professor Havens has pointed out, Blackmore has the doubtful distinction of being attacked by more illustrious pens than any minor poet in English literary history before or since.[24]

[22] W. MacNeile Dixon, *English Epic and Heroic Poetry* (London, 1912), p. 241; Hoxie Fairchild, *Religious Trends in English Poetry*, I, 1700-40 (New York, 1939), 189, n. 54.
[23] Henry Morley, *A Manual of English Literature*, revised by Moses C. Tyler (New York, 1879), p. 511.
[24] R. D. Havens, *The Influence of Milton on English Poetry* (Cambridge, Mass., 1925), p. 90.

III. THE PUBLICATION OF *COMMENDATORY VERSES* AND *DISCOMMENDATORY VERSES*

THE folio *Commendatory Verses, on the Author of the Two Arthurs, and the Satyr against Wit* made its appearance early in March, 1700, and caused a sufficient uproar to be answered, a month later, by *Discommendatory Verses, on Those Which are Truly Commendatory, on the Author of the Two Arthurs, and the Satyr against Wit.*[1]

Although almost nothing is known about the identity of the compiler of *Discommendatory Verses*, or, for that matter, the contributors to it, there is a good deal of evidence to show that Tom Brown edited *Commendatory Verses*. Most scholars simply accept that as a fact, basing their belief on an accusation in the Preface to *Discommendatory Verses*

---

[1] *Commendatory Verses* was advertised in the *Post-Boy*, issue of March 12-14; *Discommendatory Verses* was announced in the *Flying-Post* for April 16-18, though Luttrell's copy is dated April 6. For a chronological listing of the 1700 pamphlets in the controversy see Appendix B.

Commendatory Verses went through two editions; apparently there were several issues of the first: (1) 30 pages of text, with booklists at the foot of pages 28 and 30; (2) the same, with pages 18 and 19 misnumbered 14 and 15; (3) 28 pages of text, with a booklist at the foot of the page; (4) the same, with the misnumbered pages. The extra sheet contains the "Lent-Entertainment." The second edition (1702) is the same as the 30-page text described above, but with a different title page: *Commendatory Verses: Or, a Step towards a Poetical War, Betwixt Covent-Garden and Cheap-Side . . . .* For a description of the 30-page *Commendatory Verses* and the second edition, see Arthur E. Case, *Bibliography of English Poetical Miscellanies, 1521-1750* (Bibliographical Society, Oxford, 1935), Nos. 217 and 217b (pp. 155-156); for the location of these volumes see Arthur E. Case and also Richard C. Boys, "A Finding-List of English Poetical Miscellanies 1700-48 in Selected American Libraries," *ELH*, 7 (1940), 147.

and the statement in the various editions of Tom Brown's *Works* that the epigrams against Blackmore were "collected by Mr. Brown." The matter is not so simple, however, for there are several legitimate objections to Brown's editorship. For that reason, it is necessary here to reëxamine the case.

We can be reasonably sure that Brown had some part in *Commendatory Verses*. In the letter to "Sir W. S——," which is dated January 8 [1700], he speaks of the projected volume: "They talk of *Squibbing* [Blackmore] with *Epigrams*; for my part, I think 'tis doing him too much *Honour*, and making him more *considerable* than he deserves; however, if they go on with it, I shall not be wanting to contribute my *Quota* to so *Pious* a *Design*."[2] Brown was, in fact, the principal contributor to the book. The editor of *Discommendatory Verses*, whoever he was, apparently was well informed about the poets of *Commendatory Verses*, for with a few exceptions the ascriptions in *Discommendatory Verses* are verified by those given in Tom Brown's *Works*. The Preface to *Discommendatory Verses* singles out Brown for special attention, calling him the "Secretary to the Confederates at *Will's* Coffee-house." The Wits, we are told, "have chosen T—— B—— for their Leader," a move the opposition comments on:

> B——n Thou believ'st Thou'rt famous for a Jest,
> And none like Thou, for Wit, can bear the Test;
> Thou flatter'st All, on All Thou fling'st Thy Spight,
> Thus think'st Thy Company must needs delight:
> But if I speak what's Truth, though course and plain,
> Thou ne'er will't have thy Reck'ning *paid* again.

In several places in *Discommendatory Verses* the charge is made that Tom Brown, in financial difficulties,[3] was hired by Codrington to edit *Commendatory Verses*. He is advised to

---

[2] In *Works of . . . Voiture* (1701 section), p. 134.

[3] Matthew Smith, a former Jacobite, was hired by the Earl of Peterborough to spy on the Jacobites, but dissatisfied with his profits Smith then offered his information to the Duke of Shrewsbury, Peterborough's enemy. Soon both men

Give the fierce waspish Col'nel back his Gold,
Nor let thy Praise be bought, thy Lies be sold (p. 10),

and, in another poem, " To the Quibling, Drib'ling, Scribling
Poetaster, who has let himself out for Scandal to the Wits
at *Will's Coffee-House*" (p. 13), the reproach is echoed.
There is no way of disproving the accusation, which seems
plausible. We know that Brown did need money, and that
he had connections with Codrington;[4] his defense of the Wits
in the letter to "Sir W. S——," quoted at length above,
would make him all the more acceptable. Furthermore, he
had already come out several times in print against Blackmore. But, on the other hand, it should be remembered that
"most of the anonymous pieces which happened to please
the town, were fathered upon him,"[5] and that the authoritative biography of Codrington, V. T. Harlow's *Christopher
Codrington*, which contains one of the most detailed accounts
we have of the *Commendatory Verses* quarrel, does not men-
tion such an arrangement with Brown. It may be further
objected that Brown probably would not edit a volume of
prose so laudatory to Dryden, whom he had chivvied for
years. Actually, by 1700 Brown had gotten over much of
his enmity towards Dryden,[6] and no doubt he was willing
to bury in a pot of guineas any animosity that remained.
Certainly, as far as his relations with Dryden were concerned,
Brown was not hypocritical, for whatever adulation there

---

brushed him off and Smith retaliated by publishing his *Memoirs of Secret Service*
(February, 1699), where, among other things, he provoked the wrath of Richard
Kingston, a Whig pamphleteer. Kingston replied and charged that the *Memoirs*
had been edited by Tom Brown and that he had admitted his part in the book
to Abel Roper and others; Brown and Roper actually came to blows before the
episode was finished. After much bickering Kingston added a further charge
that Brown had been given an advance payment on a book he had never finished
and that he had never returned the money (Benjamin Boyce, *Tom Brown*,
pp. 122-125). Such a tale, substantiated or not, would appeal to Blackmore
and his defenders.

[4] Harlow, *Christopher Codrington*, p. 46.

[5] Shiels and Cibber, *Lives* (see p. 32, n. 8), III, 207.

[6] Benjamin Boyce, *Tom Brown*, pp. 126-127.

may be in *Commendatory Verses* is not found in Brown's own poems.

The Preface to *Commendatory Verses* is signed "O. S.," initials which, apparently, have never been identified, although a few scholars have thought that Brown wrote the introductory piece. The clue to the identity of "O. S." lies in Brown's *Works*, where an Owen Swan, vintner of the Black Swan Tavern, appears several times. In Brown's "On his friend *Owen Swan*, at the *Black-Swan Tavern*, in Bartholemew-Lane," he says that

> . . . The God of *Wine* has made
> Thee *Steward* of the gay *Carousing Trade*.[7]

He addresses Swan in another place: "You promis'd to send me some Wine, you forget your Friends. I must excuse you; *great Wits* have *short Memories*. Pray remember me to the Rakes; tell 'em I would drink their *Healths*, if you would afford me Wine, which pray send by the first Opportunity . . . ."[8] Swan's supposed reply is in the same vein, stating that "the Rakes last Night were all in bodily *Health*, and drank yours *heartily*"; he also appends a poem:

> I, *Owen Swan*, the most sincere and honest Man ⎫
> That e'er drew Wine in *Quart* or *Can*,   ⎬
> From *Beersheba* unto *Dan*,   ⎭
> Most humbly thank you for your sage Epistle:
> Tho' my Muse can't *Sing*, she'll strive to Whistle.
> Your virtuous Gentlemen, the Rakes,   ⎫
> Last Night were in for Ale and Cakes,   ⎬
> (For Wine I mean) but you'll forgive Mistakes. ⎭
> The *Wits*, dear Brother,——
> Are us'd to pardon one another;
> And may *Old Nick* your Humble take,   ⎫
> And as a Neighbour *Brews*, so may he never *Bake*, ⎬
> If he'd not drink an Ocean for your sake.   ⎭

---

[7] *Works* (1720), I, 154.

[8] "A Letter to Mr. *Owen Swan*, at the *Black-Swan* Tavern in *Bartholomew-Lane*, upon his forgetting to send Wine into the Country," in *Works* (1720), I, 229.

My Verses limp; and why? 'Tis meet
They keep Proportion to the Feet
Of him, who to his Cellar ran
To fill your Bottles,

OWEN SWAN.[9]

Owen Swan, then, emerges from these jocular pieces by Tom
Brown as the keeper of a tavern much frequented by the
Wits, and to have him "write" letters and poems would be
considered a great joke which would be relished by habitués
of the Black Swan. No doubt Tom Brown used the name of
Owen Swan as a *nom de plume* well known to the other Wits,
a simple device that would afford those convivial spirits
great amusement.

The Preface to *Commendatory Verses* makes sense in
these terms. It pretends to be addressed to city-dwellers,
tradesmen, and other members of the *bourgeoisie* who would
by temperament be friendly towards Blackmore, the City
Bard. Since Wit is the enemy, O. S. assures the citizens that
Blackmore is not contaminated by it: "he has writ twenty
thousand Verses and upwards without one Grain of Wit in
them." He is also the friend of the craftsman and "keeps
Ten Paper-mill[s] a going with his *Job* and *Habakkuk*, and
his other Hebrew Heroes." Similarly, we are told, he wrote
his Arthurian epics solely to furnish materials for trunk
makers. In short, O. S. pleads, "Fellow-Citizens, for mine,
and for your own, and your Families sakes, hug and cherish
this worthy Gentleman" and get him to make verses
"wherein he may discreetly intersperse some notable Precepts against Trusting, some pretty Touches in defence of
Usury, and some handsom Consolations for Cuckoldom . . . ."
He might also be prevailed upon to "write a few pacifying
Strains to calm the distemper'd Spirits of our Car-men, and
the Oyster-Women at Bilingsgate." One further bit of evidence which supports the hypothesis given above is that the
Preface to *Commendatory Verses* was usually included in

[9] *Ibid.*, p. 230.

Tom Brown's collected works, where it is said that it was "*suppos'd* to be written by a Citizen to his Brethren."[10] It is also possible that Brown made use of the Owen Swan device to hoax the public again in *Luctus Britannici* (1700), a poetical miscellany occasioned by Dryden's death.[11]

It is not surprising that no printer is given on the title pages of *Commendatory Verses* and *Discommendatory*

---

[10] *Ibid.*, p. 131 (my italics).

[11] *Luctus Britannici: Or the Tears of the British Muses; For the Death of John Dryden, Esq.* (1700).

The folio volume, which is " by the most Eminent Hands in the two famous *Universities*, and by several Others," is in two parts, the first fifty-five pages being devoted to English poems celebrating Dryden's death; then follows a section of twenty-four pages of Latin pieces, apparently by students in the universities. One of these is signed by " Audoenus Swan " (p. 17):

JOANNI DRYDEN *POETAE*

Tu Liquido delate Biformis in Aethere Vates,
(Olim Maeonii Carminis Ales eras.)
Accipe Cognatos fert quos Tibi *Cygnus* Honores:
Non nisi *Cygneis* Laus tua digna modis.
At Turpes absint Luctus, nam Funus inane,
Nulla supervacuo Naenia more juvat.

This is translated by Professor O. M. Pearl, of the Greek Department of the University of Michigan, as follows:

TO JOHN DRYDEN, POET

Thou, bard of double guise, upborne in shining air
(Of old the winged voice of epic lays)
Accept the kindred honors *Swan* to thee doth bear—
The modes of *Swan* alone rise to thy praise.
Yet absent the base grief, for funeral care
And needless dirge boots not the empty vase.

Here we have, on the surface, a conventional poem lamenting the death of Dryden. However, once again the authorship of the poem presents a problem. It is possible to identify the other contributors to this section as Oxonians or Cantabrigians, since, except for the authors of poems simply initialed, the poets are listed either in *Alumni Oxonienses 1500-1714* (compiled by Joseph Foster, Oxford, 1891), or in *Alumni Cantabrigienses*, Pt. 1 (to 1751, compiled by John Venn and J. A. Venn, Cambridge, 1922). No Owen Swan is given in either volume. It seems plausible that once again Tom Brown was making use of his pen name, " Owen Swan." But, it will be objected, what is Brown, who was certainly not friendly to Dryden, doing writing a poem in praise of the deceased? It would appear likely that this piece is another of Tom Brown's jokes, in which he has the tavern keeper Owen Swan pay his tribute to Dryden.

Verses, and there is no direct proof as to who did issue them. However, at the end of the second edition of *Commendatory Verses* (1702) there is a list of books sold by J. Nutt; since Nutt printed and sold several of Brown's other works it is possible that he was responsible for *Commendatory Verses* as well. The thirty-page issue, and the second edition of *Commendatory Verses*, which appeared in 1702, merely added one sheet to the original twenty-eight pages. The new poem was "A Lent Entertainment: Or, A Merry Interview by Moon-light, betwixt a Ghost and the City-Bard," which was not reprinted in Tom Brown's *Works*. Because of a resemblance between this piece and Ayloffe's "*Mr.* DRYDEN, *to the Lord* ——," in the *Letters from the Dead to the Living* (1702), the comments on the Blackmore-Wits quarrel in the latter volume probably refer to the later edition of *Commendatory Verses.*[12]

The story of the publication of *Discommendatory Verses* is shrouded in even greater mystery than that surrounding *Commendatory Verses*. Although some scholars attribute *Discommendatory Verses* entirely to Blackmore himself, it seems certain that it, too, was the fruit of several poets' labors. The best piece of evidence to this effect is found in "To a Physician in the Country, Giving a true State of the Poetical War between *Cheapside* and *Covent-Garden*," which was usually printed immediately after Tom Brown's "To Sir W. S——," quoted extensively above, and which is said to be "By Another Hand." In opening, the writer sets the scene:

"SIR,

"We are almost barren of News; the War betwixt the *Northern Crowns*, and the *Poetical Physicians* is the only Subject

---

[12] In the *Works* of Tom Brown (1720), II, 148-149. The next letter, Ayloffe's "*A Letter from Mr.* ABRAHAM COWLEY, *to the* Covent Garden SOCIETY" (pp. 149-151), also alludes to the controversy: "Can't *Arthur* be a worthless Poem, but a Squadron of Poets must tell all the World so?" The *Letters from the Dead to the Living* was advertised in the *Post-Boy* for March 12, 1702.

at present; *Holstein* and *Riga, Cheapside* and *Covent-Garden*
the Scene of all our Coffee-house Debates. What passes in
our two first, the Publick Prints will inform you; the latter
I shall endeavour to give you some Account of: You are not
Ignorant of the *Civil War* that is broke out amongst the
Subjects of *Apollo*, and what Disorders we have lately had
in *Parnassus*. Two brawny *Heroes*, the Sons of *Paean*, head
the opposite Factions; both have signalized themselves extra-
ordinarily, one in Four Poems, which he has Printed, and
to'ther in a Poem printed four times. The *City Bard* takes
Arms to drive out *Wit*, as an *Evil Councellor* from all the
Realms of *Apollo*. The *Covent-Garden Hero* rises in its
Defence, and maintains its Services. This Quarrel is so far
spread, that it's not like to be decided *Proprio Marte*; each
Chief has his Faction, the *Knight* of the *Round-Table* has
gathered a Body of Mercenaries, to whom, on the other side,
are opposed a Squadron of Auxiliary Volunteers; and thus,
as in Forty One, *Blew-Aprons*, and *Laced-Coats* are drawn
up against one another, and the *Rabble* and *Gentlemen* set
together by the Ears; each side confident of Success, that
trusting to their Multitudes, this to their Courage and Con-
duct. The *Pestle* and *Mortar-men* are drawn up against the
Æsculapian-Band; the first, who like *Taylors* and *Women*
measure the Goodness of every Thing by the length, assert
the good old Cause of long *Bills*, and long *Poems*, against
the *Jus Divinum* of Efficacy and Sense; and think it infinitely
more Meritorious to write three or four *Folio's* without Wit,
than to fill a small *Octavo* with it, and prefer the Art of
Swelling a *Bill*, before the *Skill* to *Cure* a *Disease*. The
Cheapside Hero, they say, devoted himself wholly to their
Service, and *Rhimes* as well as Prescribes to the use of their
Shops: However, this doubty Chief, in the midst of his
Cheapside Triumphs, has been brought under Martial Disci-
pline, and forc'd to run the Gantlet in *Covent-Garden*, and
switch'd through the whole Posse of *Parnassus*, for fighting
against the Law of Arms with false Colours, Those that
favour his Cause complain of the Injustice and Indignity of
his Punishment, alledging, he suffers for what he never did.
They on the other Hand defend their Proceedings, and affirm

they know him through his Disguise, and that coming upon 'em in Masquerade, he ought to suffer as a *Spy*, or an *Assassin*, and deserves no more Quarter, than he gives to his *Patients*. Notwithstanding this, his Party have rallied once more, and the *Mercenaries* are brought to the Attack, who hope to effect that by Stratagem, that they despair of by plain Force; and, like the *Scots* at the *Bass*, since they can't reduce 'em by *Arms*, attempt to Poison them with *Stink-Pots*. At the Head of those, is a Mendicant *Rhymer*, one that begs with a *Poem*, like a *Pass* in his Hand, and with a *Sham Brief*, as a Sufferer by *Poetick Fire*, has Collected the Charity of well-disposed Persons through all *Parnassus* for above twice Twelve *Months*; and like a true Beggar, when he has tired 'em out, falls a Railing: For a Bribe from his Ballad-Printer's not large enough to Rob him of the Benefit of the Act of Parliament, for the Relief of Poor Prisoners; and the Promise of a Dinner now and then from Sir *Arthur*, he has consented to *Libel* his Benefactors, and return to his old Quarters, and subsist for the Remainder of his Life upon the *Basket*. Thus countenanced and encouraged, he lays about him most desperately, and like one not much concern'd for the Success, draws his *Incense*, and *Ammunition* from the same *House* of *Office*. *Friends* and *Foes* are treated alike in Compliment, he Paints one with the same Sir-reverence, that he aims to bedaub the other; and when his Hand is in, like the Conqueror in *Hudibrass*'s Ovation, bestows his Ordure very liberally amongst the Spectators. Thus, Sir, I have given you a true Account of the State of the *Poetical War*, headed on both Sides by Gentlemen of your Faculty; among whom, though here has been no Bloodshed, there has been as much Noise of Slaughter and Execution, as in *Holstein*, or *Livonia*. You may expect more on the same Subject, for the Quarrel is not like to drop, while *Hopkins* can tell his Fingers, or *Wesley* subsists on *Mumping in Metre*."[13]

It would seem clear that Blackmore had marshaled his forces: ". . . Each Chief has his Faction, the *Knight* of the *Round-Table* has gathered a Body of Mercenaries . . . .   His

[13] *Works of . . . Voiture*, 1701 section, pp. 136-140.

Party have rallied once more, and the *Mercenaries* are brought to the Attack . . . . At the Head of those, is a Mendicant *Rhymer* . . . ." The identity of this " Rhymer " is unknown.[14]

[14] The editor of *Discommendatory Verses* would seem to be a person friendly to Blackmore and we immediately think of someone like Watts, Defoe, Samuel Wesley. But there is no evidence that any one of these was directly mixed up in the polemics of *Commendatory Verses*; although Defoe might conceivably have sanctioned some of the scurrilous poems in *Discommendatory Verses*, it seems unlikely that Wesley or Watts would have done so. Furthermore, Defoe is not attacked in *Commendatory Verses*. Similarly, the ponderous scholar Bentley would hardly be described as " a Mendicant Rhymer," nor would he have much to gain as editor of *Discommendatory Verses*, for he had already put Boyle and the Wits to flight—to his own satisfaction, at any rate. Collier and Rymer do not fit the mould either, unless the " Mendicant *Rhymer* " is a play on the latter's name. " To a Physician in the Country " tells us that this unknown editor is a hack who has " Collected the Charity of well-disposed Persons through all *Parnassus* for above twice Twelve *Months* " (*Works of . . . Voiture*, 1701 section, p. 139). He has also " consented to *Libel his Bene-factors . . . . Friends* and *Foes* are treated alike . . . ." He does not, then, have to be in Blackmore's camp at all. " To a Physician," in describing the fight, says that " thus, as in Forty One, *Blew-Aprons*, and *Laced Coats* are drawn up against one another " (p. 137), and " To Sir W. S—— " names Samuel Cobb as a " Blew-Coat Boy " (*Works of . . . Voiture*, 1701 section, p. 135). In the same letter Cobb's *Poetae Britannici* is linked with Blackmore's *Satyr against Wit*, by Brown. On the other hand, Cobb is nowhere lampooned in *Commendatory Verses*. Cobb also attacked Blackmore a few years later, in his *Poems on Several Occasions* (1707, pp. 213-214). Evidently both sides had a fairly good idea of the identity of the enemy's forces, as we can see from the replies in *Discommendatory Verses*, and it hardly seems likely that Cobb would have escaped unscathed had he edited *Discommendatory Verses*. It is unfortunate that *Discommendatory Verses* was not answered by a new edition of *Commendatory Verses* (the second edition of *Commendatory Verses* is merely a reprinting of the original edition with a new title page).

IV. AUTHORSHIP OF THE POEMS

ALL the poems in *Commendatory Verses* and *Discommendatory Verses* are anonymous, though by the use of external evidence it is possible to identify most of the poets who participated in the first volume; the roster includes some of the best-known writers of the day, such as Sedley, Steele, and Tom Brown. With a few exceptions the poems in *Commendatory Verses* were not later reprinted in the collected works of the various authors. Certainly the quality of the poems is not high, which may account for the poets' reluctance to claim the pieces. And, as the battle of *Commendatory Verses* was not a particularly creditable one, it is easy to imagine a man like Steele wishing in later life to forget the whole unsavory episode.

There are two principal sources for our knowledge of the authorship of the poems in *Commendatory Verses*, namely, the various editions of Tom Brown's *Works* and *Discommendatory Verses*. The contributors to the latter apparently knew who their enemies were, and there are many references to specific writers in that volume.[1] Obligingly enough, most of the poems in *Commendatory Verses* were later included in Brown's *Works*, where the editor was kind enough to give

---

[1] Although the names are not always identifiable, they usually are, being but thinly disguised in the accepted manner of the day. The practice is described in the *Spectator*, No. 567 (July 14, 1714): "Some of our authors, indeed, when they would be more satyrical than ordinary, omit only the vowels of a great man's name, and fall most unmercifully upon all the consonants. This way of writing was first of all introduced by T—m Br—wn of facetious memory, who, after having gutted a proper name of all its intermediate vowels, used to plant it in his works, and make as free with it as he pleased."

the authors' names in most cases. With a few exceptions the ascriptions in the *Works* agree with those in *Discommendatory Verses*; the poems by Brown himself are found in Volume I, while those by other hands usually appear in Volume IV.

Although a detailed examination of the problems of authorship in *Commendatory Verses* is given in Appendix A, a few comments about the chief contributors are in order here. Tom Brown "of facetious memory" was the Prince of Grub Street. His personal inclinations and the need for money made him ideally suited for the job of editing *Commendatory Verses*. A prolific writer in his own right, Brown had no hesitation about contributing several of his own verses to the collection. Nearly a quarter of the poems are his. Next to Tom Brown, the man who had the largest share in the volume was Christopher Codrington, who is referred to as "Codron" throughout. By profession a soldier, Codrington was already Governor-General of the Leeward Islands, but in 1700 he was a leader of the Christ Church Wits and a friend of Tom Brown's.[2] Sir Samuel Garth was also a close acquaintance, and for the third edition of the *Dispensary* he asked Codrington and a few others to write some commendatory verses. Codrington's "To My Friend the Author" is the only work of his which has survived in eighteenth-century anthologies.[3]

Since Codrington, Brown, and the other Wits had come to his defense in the fight over the Dispensary, it was only natural that Garth should tilt a lance at Blackmore in *Commendatory Verses*, which is full of echoes of the Dispensary quarrel. By some, Garth was considered the leader of the Wits, as the following lines from the *Epistle to Sr. Richard Blackmore* (1700) show:

> Tho *Con[greve]* may in time, when he has merit,
> The Prophet's [Dryden's] Throne in peaceful sway inherit,

---

[2] Harlow, *Christopher Codrington*, p. 46.   [3] *Ibid.*, p. 92.

> The Poets all with one consent agree
> His mantle falls to G[arth] by Destiny,
> Who did whilst living wear his Livery (p. 8).

As a person Garth seems to have been almost universally liked by his contemporaries, and Dr. Harvey Cushing's praise in our own day shows that his profession still thinks well of him.[4] A member of the genial Kit-Cats, Garth could write on a serious subject, as he did in the *Dispensary* (which was widely read for fifty years), or on more trifling matters. "He wrote verses easily, and some, preserved in manuscript, were certainly intended to be read only by men far advanced in post-prandial potations," says one biographer, Mr. Norman Moore.[5] No doubt many of the verses in *Commendatory Verses* were written by poets at Will's while in this blissful condition.

Although John Dennis's rôle in *Commendatory Verses* has not been definitely established, it is likely that he was a contributor.[6] His part in the quarrel needs clarification, however, for by temperament he should have been aligned with Blackmore, not against him. It is difficult for us to imagine him rollicking with men like Tom Brown at Will's, but for a time he did. Nor was he without his reward, for in 1700 Codrington and his friends supported Dennis's unsuccessful play, *Iphigenia*. After 1700 Dennis withdrew from clubs and coteries and, not many years later, gave expression to his true feelings about such cliques: "Who that has Common-sense can forbear laughing, when he sees a Parcel of Fellows, who call themselves Wits, sit in Combination round a Coffee Table, as Sharpers do round a Hazard Table, to trick honest Gentlemen into an Approbation of their Works, and bubble them of their understandings?"[7] He complained bitterly about "those thousand *extempore* [lampoons], which are

---

[4] In "Dr. Garth, Kit-Cat Poet," in the *Bulletin of the Johns Hopkins Hospital*, 17, No. 178 (January, 1906), 1-17.

[5] *DNB*, XXI, 31.

[6] *Dennis*, ed. Hooker, II, xviii.

[7] *Ibid.*, II, 174 (Dennis to Steele, Sept. 4, 1719); see also II, xlvi.

hourly utter'd by Club and Coffee-house Gentlemen, *Petty Merchants of small Conceits*, as my late Lord *Hallifax* calls them . . . .[8] Obviously Dennis had had a change of heart since the turbulent days of *Commendatory Verses*!

Good fellowship around the punchbowl at Will's does not, however, go far to explain Dennis's part in *Commendatory Verses*, for there seems little doubt that his antagonism to Blackmore was purely a matter of literary criticism and not the outgrowth of personal animosity. He had much in common with his adversary; both were supporters of the King, both by nature disliked the frivolous goings-on of the Wits, both believed vehemently in the power of religion. The air was soon cleared between the two after the appearance of *Commendatory Verses*. In 1704 Blackmore was a subscriber to Dennis's critical work; by 1716 Dennis was carrying on an amiable correspondence with the knight; in 1717 Dennis was hailing Blackmore as a rival to Lucretius, and, returning the compliment, in 1723 Blackmore was placing Dennis above Boileau in critical abilities.[9] If we find it difficult to reconcile such a love feast with the harsh words of *Commendatory Verses*, we should not forget that frequently the critic in Dennis made him utter harsh words which did not agree with his personal feelings. Another case in point is Dryden, whom Dennis defended passionately on the one hand and criticized on the other.[10] His honesty as a critic can account for such a state of affairs, but frequently Dennis's irascibility made him do an about-face, thus creating confused situations which, incidentally, are an important part of *Commendatory Verses* in general. For example, Thomas Cheek, himself possibly a contributor to *Commendatory Verses*, was Dennis's friend in the 1690's, but won his enmity by writing a Prologue for Abel Boyer's *Achilles*, a rival to Dennis's play, *Iphigenia*. The *Letters of Wit*, in which Cheek and Boyer

---

[8] *Ibid.*, II, 397 (from the *Essay upon Publick Spirit*, 1711).
[9] *Ibid.*, I, 448.   [10] *Ibid.*, II, xiv-xv.

had a hand, were also critical of Dennis, though Boyer later became more friendly.[11] Similarly, Steele later became Blackmore's admirer, as did Addison (whom Blackmore had attacked in the *Satyr against Wit*).[12]

Other important literary figures who had a part in *Commendatory Verses* were Charles Boyle, whose rôle has already been discussed, Steele (defending his friend Addison), and Sir Charles Sedley. Sedley may have been stirred to action because he was ignored in the *Satyr against Wit*, for, as far as the Wits were concerned, to be attacked by Blackmore was a sure measure of poetic success. The list of *Commendatory Verses* poets also includes the following: the Earl of Anglesea, Col. Henry Blount, Dr. James Drake, Col. Johnson, Francis Manning, Mildmay, Richard Norton, the Countess of Sandwich, and Dr. Thomas Smith. Others who may have written poems for the volume were: Dr. Edward Baynard, Nicholas Brady, William Burnaby, Thomas Cheek, Thomas Creech, Knightly Chetwood, Anthony Henley, William

---

[11] *Ibid.*, II, xix-xx.

[12] The unpredictability of the cross fire in the controversy is reflected in the relationship between Addison and Blackmore. In spirit the two had much in common; not many years before *Commendatory Verses* Addison was certainly on speaking terms with Blackmore, as can be seen from the following statement: " I was yesterday with Dr. Hannes and communicated your Request to him. I told him y^t Dr Blackmore, Mr Adams, Mr Boyle & myself had Engag'd in it & that you had gaind a kind of Promise from Dr Gibbons, so that he cou'd not plead Want of Time " (Addison to Jacob Tonson, in the *Letters of Joseph Addison*, ed. Walter Graham, Oxford, 1941, pp. 1-2). This letter, which refers to a proposed edition of Herodotus, poses several problems: (1) If this letter is to be dated 1695, as Graham suggests, what are Boyle and Addison, particularly Boyle, doing in the company of Blackmore and Gibbons, both of whom Boyle and his friends later attacked in *Commendatory Verses*? Boyle had already, in 1694, declared war on Bentley, whose cause was taken up in *Discommendatory Verses* by Blackmore six years later. (2) Is Graham's date of 1695 for this letter acceptable? Certainly it seems unlikely that it was written before that year, for Blackmore had no reputation as a literary man until 1695. On the other hand, would Boyle, one of the leaders of the Wits, risk ridicule at the hands of his friends by collaborating with Blackmore? Possibly the resentment against Blackmore had not yet reached an explosive stage; it was not until 1696 that Dennis's *Remarks on . . . Prince Arthur* appeared; the *Satyr against Wit*, which goaded the Wits into replying in kind, did not reach the reading public until 1699.

Walsh, Lord Mordaunt, John Sheffield, Dr. Smalwood, and Sir Henry Sheeres. The absence of certain names from this list, particularly Congreve's, invites comment. Many looked on Congreve as Dryden's successor to the pontifical throne at Will's:

> His mighty Dr[yde]n to the Shades is gone,
> And Con[gre]ve leaves successor of his Throne . . . .
> Heir to his Plays, his Fables and his Tales,
> Con[greve] is the *Poetick Prince of Wales*;
> Not at the Germain's but at *Will*'s his Court,
> Whither the Subjects of his Dad resort.[13]

As a leading member of the group which Blackmore spoke scathingly of in the *Satyr against Wit*, Congreve might well have joined the pack, but he did not. Possibly the answer lies in the Preface to *King Arthur* (pp. vii-viii), where Blackmore goes out of his way to praise *The Mourning Bride* and exonerate its author from the charge of immorality. Even in the more pointed *Satyr against Wit* Blackmore is content with merely chiding Congreve gently for straying from the paths of virtue. Then, too, by 1700 Congreve was already beginning to drift away from the bustle of literary London, and he may well have wanted to keep clear of the wrangling.

This survey of authorship and that in Appendix A are by no means completely conclusive, for undoubtedly as new evidence turns up the picture will change in details. Yet it seems reasonably certain that the general pattern will remain as it is. That the problem of authorship is in many ways the most baffling aspect of *Commendatory Verses* is seen, for in the fact that V. T. Harlow adds several names to the list of authors: George Markham, Col. Stanhope, Clotwood, Adams, Dr. Morley, Lord Carbury, and Arthur Mainwaring.[14] I have found no evidence which would link up

---

[13] *Epistle to Sr. Richard Blackmore, occasion'd by the new session of the Poets*, p. 7.

[14] *Christopher Codrington*, p. 232, n. 2. Robert M. Krapp adds Luke Milbourne's name to the list of contributors (*Science and Society*, 10 [1946], 89).

these writers with *Commendatory Verses*, though some are likely candidates. Professor V. de Sola Pinto mentions a British Museum copy of *Commendatory Verses* which has the authors' names written in in a contemporary hand.[15] While such evidence is never completely authoritative, it is certainly useful, and this volume, when it is available, may supply the missing information. One thing is sure: if the proof of authorship presented in this study is at all acceptable, there are not enough poems left over for all of the additional authors.

[15] *Poetical and Dramatic Works of Sir Charles Sedley*, I, xvii.

V. THE CONTENTS OF *COMMENDATORY VERSES*

THE details of Blackmore's life before the publication of *Commendatory Verses* do not concern us here. Born in Wiltshire about 1650, he was educated at Westminster and Oxford, took his medical degree at Padua, and settled in London to practice. An early supporter of the Bloodless Revolution, he was rewarded with a knighthood and made a physician to William, a professional position he also held under Queen Anne. He died on October 9, 1729. The malicious poems in *Commendatory Verses* are directed at half a dozen vulnerable spots in his early life. When a young man, Blackmore had tried his hand at schoolteaching. It is difficult to see why this should give rise to such mirth on the part of the Wits (for some of the contributors to *Commendatory Verses* had also taught), but it plays an important part in the poems. The opening lines of the miscellany were widely quoted:

> By Nature meant, by Want a Pedant made,
> Bl[ackmo]re at first profess'd the Whipping Trade (p. 1).

Throughout the volume, the poets of *Commendatory Verses* monotonously repeat the charges in the following lines:

> By whipping Boys your Cruelty began,
> And grew by bolder Steps to killing Man (p. 16).

It was inevitable that Blackmore's ability as a doctor should also be called in question; indeed, this was true of all the medical men on both sides of the controversy, Garth, Gibbons, Sloane, Smith, Drake, and others. The Dispensary squabble was, of course, at the bottom of the invective, but added to this was a feeling on the part of the Wits that a doctor should leave poetry to poets [1] (it was evidently proper for Garth and Drake to write, for they were on the side of the angels). Blackmore himself was responsible for at least part of this attack, as we have already seen in the naïve Preface he wrote for *Prince Arthur*. The scoffing assumed a definite pattern, which is echoed throughout *Commendatory Verses*. Garth (p. 4), with a fine disregard for professional ethics, tells Blackmore that "thy Poems, and thy Patients live not long" and Boyle claims (p. 3) that "his Satyr Wounds not, but his Physick kills."

> We bid thee not give o'er the Killing Trade:
> Whilst Fees come in, 'tis fruitless to diswade,

adds the Earl of Anglesea (p. 7), introducing the mercenary note. Sedley's lines are perhaps the best in the whole volume:

> It is a common Pastime to write Ill;
> And Doctor, with the rest e'en take thy fill.
> Thy Satyr's harmless: 'Tis thy Prose that kills,
> When thou Prescrib'st thy Potions, and thy Pills (p. 2).

That the charge of mixing poetry and medicine was a common one leveled against Blackmore can be seen from the following quotation taken from another contemporary critic: "Who can without concern, observe every Year large Books of Poetry publish'd, to procure a Reputation in Medicine?

---

[1] The pitfalls which lie in the path of the poet-doctor are well expressed by Dr. Harvey Cushing (*Bulletin of the Johns Hopkins Hospital*, 17, No. 178 [January, 1906], 11): "Few indeed have been the disciples of Aesculapius who have climbed the severe ascent of high Parnassus, and at the same time been faithful to their vocation. Too often has this divided allegiance meant the unqualified sacrifice of Physic upon the shrine of the Corycian nymphs: for the public has ever been shy of the physician who allows his mind to soar above the level of most practical and mundane things, and a genius so inclined, has, in reciprocation, not uncommonly failed of success in his profession from an equal shyness of the public."

Poetry of the Heroick Style, is too Noble to be made a Procuress for Practice."[2]

The Wits felt they had another source of ridicule in their claim that Blackmore had won his knighthood and his appointment as a King's physician through his efforts as epic poet in *King Arthur,* an accusation which is probably justified.[3] Certainly Blackmore, following in the Spenserian tradition, draws an obvious, if somewhat forced, parallel between the England of Arthur and the England of William. Arthur is, of course, William, and both are champions of Protestant Christendom. There are clear references to Louis XIV, the taking of Namur, and the Peace of Ryswick, and Arthur-William is successful in relieving the suffering of the Protestants in France under Louis. The allegory is thinly disguised: "Sakil" is Sackville, "Trelon," Trelawney, and so on, a fact which the Wits gleefully pointed out:

> With mangled Names old Stories he pollutes,
> And to the present Time past Action suits;
> Amaz'd we find, in ev'ry Page he writes,
> Members of Parliament with *Arthur's* Knights (p. 2).

So pleased was the seventeenth-century Arthur with the epics that Blackmore was knighted early in 1696.[4]

The Wits lost no time in probing the sore spot of Blackmore's professional advancement:

> Knighthood to Hero's only once was due,
> Now's the Reward of stupid Praise in you.
> Why shou'd a Quack be dubb'd, unless it be
> That pois'ning is an Act of Chivalry? (p. 16)

Nor was Blackmore's obsequiousness, they jeeringly went on, confined to his dealings with the King, for in the epics and

---

[2] *Homer and Virgil not to be Compar'd with the Two Arthurs* (1700), pp. 75-76.

[3] Roberta F. Brinkley, *Arthurian Legend in the Seventeenth Century* (see p. 16, n. 17), p. 185.

[4] See *ibid.,* pp. 175-185.

the *Satyr against Wit* Blackmore tried to curry favor with influential nobles of the land. Sedley put his finger on this weakness:

> A Grave Physician us'd to write for Fees,
> And spoil no Paper, but with Recipe's,
> Is now turn'd Poet, rails against all Wit,
> Except that Little found among the Great (p. 2).

Another of Blackmore's great misfortunes, as the Wits saw it, was to live in Cheapside, while they clustered in the more fashionable section of London. "City Dweller" was a term of scorn, and Blackmore is frequently known as the "City Bard." The Knight's sympathizer, Jeremy Collier, reminds us that citizens had long been the butt of jokes on the Restoration stage; "[In comedy] the rich Citizens are often Misers and Cuckolds . . . ,"[5] a tradition which Steele was attempting to break in his *Conscious Lovers*, as late as 1722, by making a merchant one of the heroes of his play. Of Blackmore's issuing the *Satyr against Wit* anonymously, Steele writes in *Commendatory Verses*:

> In vain thou woud'st thy Name, dull Pedant, hide,
> There's not a Line but smells of thy *Cheapside* (p. 5).

And the Countess of Sandwich says that only "Cits and pious Ladies lik'd thy Stuff" (p. 7).

When Blackmore was unwise enough, in the Preface to *King Arthur*, to admit that he often composed his verses as he went about the streets making calls on patients, he furnished the Wits with more material for satire. Dennis early made reference to this habit, in his Prologue to *A Plot and No Plot* (1697):

> A place [Exchange Alley] of late to Epick Muse well known,
> Perhaps that 'twas compos'd in's Coach he'd own,
> But alas poor Devil he has none.[6]

---

[5] *Short View of the Immorality and Profaneness of the English Stage* (1698), p. 145.

[6] Reprinted in *Dennis*, ed. Hooker, II, 387.

The Arthur epics were written, says Codrington, by Black-more "mounted on a Cart, whose hideous Rumbling made *Apollo* start " (p. 1) , an idea echoed by Tom Brown:

> As rattling Coach once thunder'd through the Mire,
> Out dropt Abortive *Arthur* from his Sire (p. 13) .

Blackmore's coach as the seat of the muses became a stock joke in his own day, but it is surprising to find the story kept alive well into the nineteenth century, when Tom Moore wrote:

> 'Twas in his carriage the sublime
> Sir Richard Blackmore used to rhyme;
> And (if the wits don't do him wrong),
> 'Twixt death and epics passed his time,
> Scribbling and killing all day long—
> Like Phoebus in his car, at ease,
> Now warbling forth a lofty song,
> Now murdering the young Niobes.[7]

After devoting some attention to Blackmore as the self-confessed champion of virtue and religion, the poets of *Commendatory Verses* acidly comment on his poetical works. Blackmore, says Codrington,

> . . . At length has hit
> On Bus'ness for his matchless Talent fit,
> To give us Drenches for the Plague of Wit (p. 2) .

As might be expected, more attention is given to the *Satyr against Wit* than to any of Blackmore's other works. For one thing, it was newer, having come from the press only a few months before the lines in *Commendatory Verses* appeared; it also struck more personally and bitterly than had even the Preface to *King Arthur*. The epics, however, were not overlooked:

> Spontaneous Crops of *Jobs* and *Arthurs* rise,
> Whose tow'ring Non-sense braves the very Skies:

---

[7] "Rhymes on the Road," in *The Poetical Works of Thomas Moore*, ed. David Herbert (Boston and New York, 1872), p. 233.

> Like Paper-kites the empty Volumes fly,
> And by meer force of Wind are rais'd on high . . . (p. 20).

Blackmore's offence was that he

> Burlesqu'd the Bravest, Wisest son of *Mars*
> In Ballad-rhimes, and all the Pomp of Farce (p. 1).

If one views the matter objectively it must be admitted that Blackmore's enemies seldom achieved a high level of poetic composition; they certainly lacked the lightness of touch which is so marked in the biting satires of the later *Anti-Jacobin.* Obviously they were more interested in being scathing than in writing immortal epigrams. When Sedley declared:

> Thy Satyr's harmless: 'Tis thy Prose that kills,
> When thou Prescrib'st thy Potions, and thy Pills (p. 2),

his versifying was certainly no better than Blackmore's in his *Satyr against Wit* where, speaking of Codrington, he wrote

> By Hearsay he's a Scholar, and they say
> The Man's a sort of Wit too in his way (p. 11).

In fact, the quality of *Discommendatory Verses* as a whole is as high as that of *Commendatory Verses,* which makes it difficult for the modern reader to give the Wits unqualified credit for driving the City Bard into disrepute.

* * * * *

Today, a little more than two hundred years after his death, Sir Richard Blackmore is receiving more attention than at any other time since his bumbling antagonisms caused a stir on Parnassus. This interest is occasioned not by any rediscovery of hidden poetic merit—if anything, his stock is lower than ever in that direction—but by the realization that he played a small though important part in the great social struggle which eventually resulted in the firm establishment of bourgeois ideals in literature as well as in society. Perhaps the Wits were uneasily aware of this threat when they answered his popgun assault with heavy mortar fire; certainly the *mores* that Blackmore stood for threatened the kind of life they cherished. Ridiculous as it may have seemed to the habitués of Will's Coffee House at the time, the less vocal followers of Quarles, Bunyan, Baxter, Collier, and Blackmore were, by sheer determined if unspectacular opposition, able to make their voices heard. One modern writer sees in the struggle an attempt "to alter the literary codes and canons of the day from conformity with a predominantly aristocratic, to conformity with a predominantly middle-class ideal," a movement led, at the turn of the eighteenth century by Blackmore, Defoe, and Samuel Wesley.[8] But whether the clash is thought of as a conflict between the aristocrat and the plebeian or the sophisticate and the unworldly, or the refined and the vulgar, or the godly and those who scoffed at religion, critics today are becoming increasingly aware that the controversy which raged over the publication of *Commendatory Verses* was more than the mere chastisement of a bad poet by those whose literary standards were, they thought, higher. Perhaps our fondness for such a strongly sociological approach to literary criticism leads us as far away from a true perspective as Rymer's angry insistence on the infallible rules led him, but at any rate our renewed interest in Blackmore[9] is slowly making sure that he will no longer be dismissed as ridiculous and inconsequential.

[8] Robert M. Krapp, "Class Analysis of a Literary Controversy," *Science and Society*, 10 (Winter, 1946), 81. What a shock it would have been to one of Blackmore's admirers, Dr. Johnson, to know that Blackmore would one day be defended in a publication which not long ago was listed as a "Marxian Quarterly"!

[9] Within the past decade at least two proposed doctoral theses on Blackmore have been announced. Mr. Krapp's interesting article, E. Hudson Long's "Notes on Sir Richard Blackmore" (*MLN*, 58 [1943], 585-588), and the reprinting of Blackmore's "Essay upon Wit" in the Augustan Reprint Society's publication (May, 1946) are evidence of the growing attention to Blackmore.

VI. THE TEXTS OF *COMMENDATORY VERSES* AND *DISCOMMENDATORY VERSES*

SINCE the poems in *Discommendatory Verses* are, with few exceptions, replies to specific poems in *Commendatory Verses*, the pieces are grouped here according to their relationship with the other poems. It is hoped that readability and continuity will be of greater value in tracing the development of the controversy than the reprinting of the two volumes separately would be. All footnotes, unless otherwise designated, are mine. In the two Prefaces I have reversed the roman and italic type of the originals.

CV Preface (pp. i-ii)

To all the Honourable CITIZENS within the Bills of Mortality, below the Dignity of Common-council-men.

Fellow CITIZENS,

I am no Orator, I own it, nor ever made a Speech in my Life, but once in the Vestry, about choosing a Lecturer, and new Lettering the Church-Buckets: but this I'll be bold to say, That no Man is a heartier Well-wisher to the Prosperity of this Protestant City than my self. Now I must tell you, Gentlemen, that you don't take so much Notice of a certain Author, who does you the Honour to reside among you, as his great Qualities deserve. You only consult him as a Physician; and indeed I must needs say he is a pretty Physician; He has eas'd many of you of those heavy Burdens, call'd Wives and Children; and, out of his Zeal to the Pub-

61

lick, has helpt to thin the overstock of Traders: But still you must give me leave to tell you, that you overlook his principal Talent, for Physick is what he values himself least upon. He is a Poet, pray be not scandalized at the Word, he is a Poet, I say, but of sober solid Principles, and as hearty an Enemy to Wit as the best of you all: he has writ twenty thousand Verses and upwards without one Grain of Wit in them; nay, he has declar'd open War against it, and, despising it in himself, is resolved not to endure it in any one else. When he is in his Coach, instead of pretending to read where he can't see, as some Doctors do; or thinking of his Patient's case, which none of them do, he is still listning to the Chimes, to put his Ear in tune, and stumbles upon a Distich every Kennel he is jolted over. Nay, even in Coffeehouses, when other People are cleansing *Chester*-Harbour, banishing Popish Priests, disposing the Crown of *Spain*, repairing *Dover*-Peer, pitying the poor *Scots* at *Darien*, or settling the Affairs of *Poland*, he is enditing Heroics on the back of a News-Paper with his Pencil, and wou'd give more for a Rhime to *Radziouski* than a Specific for the Gout. Those flashy Fellows, your *Covent-garden* Poets, are good for nothing, but to run into our Debts, lye with our Wives, and break unmannerly Jests upon us as Citizens; then, like a parcel of Sots, they write for Fame and Immortality; but this Gentleman is above such Trifles, and, as he prescribes, so he writes for the Good of Trade. He's a particular Benefactor to the Manufacture of the Nation; and, at this present Minute, to my certain knowledge, keeps Ten Paper-mill[s] a going with his *Job* and *Habakkuk*, and his other *Hebrew* Heroes. There's scarce a Cook, Grocer, or Tobacconist within the City-Walls but is the better for his Works; nay, one that is well acquainted with his Secret History, has assured me, that his main design in writing the two *Arthurs*, whatever he pretended in his Preface, was only to help the poor Trunkmakers at a Pinch, when *Quarles* and *Ogilby*[1] were all spent

---

[1] Probably John Quarles (1624-65), son of the better-known Francis, who

and they wanted other Materials. Above all, you can't imagine what a singular Deference he pays to a golden Chain; 'tis impossible for a rich Man with him, either to be a Knave or a Blockhead: he never sees the Cap of Maintenance, but is ready to worship it; and, in compliment to the Sword-bearer, wou'd, I dare engage for him, sooner write a Panegyric upon Custard, than any of the Cardinal Virtues, tho' he pretends to be their Champion.

This may serve, Fellow-Citizens, to give you some Idea of the Man; but what we most want his Assistance in, is to reform several enormous Abuses that have crept in among us. *The Poetry of our* Bell-men, *which in its first institution contain'd many excellent Lessons of Piety,* is grown very *loose and immoral,* and gives our Wives and Daughters wicked Ideas, when it awakes them at Midnight. The Tobacco-boxes too *seem engag'd in a general Confederacy to bring Vice into esteem;* their lewd Inscriptions *charge Religion with desperate Resolution, and have given it many deep and ghastly Wounds.* Our Posies for Rings *are either immodest, or irreligious;* and we *see few Verses* on our Ale-house-Signs, but *have some spiteful and envious Strokes at Sobriety and Good-manners, whence the* Apprentices of this Populous City *have apparently received very bad Impressions.* 'Tis great Pity that our Magistrates, *in whose Power it is, have not yet restrained the Licentiousness of* these Rhimes, *and obliged the Writers of them to observe more Decorum.* But, since they are so remiss in their Duty, retain this Gentleman *on the side of Religion,* and you'll soon see these Enormities Vanish. Besides, being of a goodly Person, if you desired him now and then, upon a Solemn Occasion, to walk before a Pageant, or march at the Head of the Blew-coat Infantry, at the Burial of one of his own Patients, with how much more Decency and Gravity wou'd those Public Ceremonies be perform'd? And then who so proper to inflame

was a prolific writer. John Ogilby (1600-76), writer of heroic poems, was ridiculed by Dryden in *MacFlecknoe.*

the Courages of our City-Militia, as our Parson tells me, one *Tyrtaeus*[2] did of old, by the Repetition of his own Lines? Well, cou'd I but be so happy as to see him once appear in the Front of our *Finsbury*-Squadrons,[3] or animate with his noble Compositions the Wrestlers in *Moor-fields*,[4] I shou'd not doubt to see our ancient Military Genius come in Play, and every *London* 'Prentice able to worst his Brace of Lions. Therefore, Fellow-Citizens, for mine, for your own, and your Families sakes, hug and cherish this worthy Gentleman, make him free of all your Companies, for he's as well qualified for any of them as his own; carry him to all your Entertainments, nay even to your private Deliberations over Brawn and Quest-ale, and when any foreign Ambassador is treated by the City, get him to pay the Compliment in Verse, and the R-c-rd-r may second him in Prose; put the entire Management of *Smithfield*[5] into his Hands, and make him absolute Monarch of all the Booths and Poppet-shews. Above all, let him endeavour by the Melody of his Rhimes (and what can withstand 'em?) to call back our fugitive Mercers from *Covent-garden* to *Ludgate-hill* and *Paternoster-row*. Since we are for new Painting our City-gates, why should we not Furbish up our old Heroes in new Metre? Why should poor King *Lud* and his two trusty Sons, *Temancus* and *Androgeus*,[6] be forgotten? Or what harm have the Giants at *Guild-hall*[7] and *Whittington's* Cat done to be buried in

[2] Tyrtaeus, a Spartan poet, during the second Messenian war (*c.* 650 B.C.) inspired the soldiers with his own lines.

[3] The Finsbury Artillery Ground was used for training troops.

[4] Moorfields was the scene of a fair; Pepys (June 28, 1661) mentions wrestling there.

[5] Where Bartholomew Fair was held.

[6] The mythical King Lud is supposed to have been responsible for many of London's buildings, including Ludgate, said to have been erected sixty-six years before the birth of Christ. (See John Stow, *Survey of London*, 1598; Everyman's Library, 1912, pp. 3-4.)

[7] Gog and Magog, which were first made of pasteboard and wicker, were carried in the pageant procession on the Lord Mayor's Day. The figures were destroyed in the Great Fire but were replaced in 1708 by copies made of wood.

oblivion? There are a thousand other Subjects to employ his Muse, wherein he may discreetly intersperse some notable Precepts against Trusting, some pretty Touches in defence of Usury, and some handsom Consolations for Cuckoldom, all which might be of admirable use to season and confirm our City-Youth in the true Principles of their Ancestors: And what if you cou'd perswade him to write a few pacifying Strains to calm the distemper'd Spirits of our Car-men and the Oyster-women at *Bilingsgate*? In short, these are some of the Topics you may recommend to him. Let him make Verses for us Citizens, and prescribe Physic to the Fools without *Temple-bar*. I am,

> *Your Loving Friend,*
> *O[wen] S[wan].*

DV Preface (pp. i-ii)

As it requires not much Thought to find out the Author of the Dedication to the Commendatory Verses, so there is no necessity of much Pains to return an Answer to it. Since Falsities are known to People who are unprejudic'd by their first appearance, and there is occasion for no other Method to find 'em out, than a true knowledge of the Gentleman who is abus'd. The Dedicator has long since been conversant in Scandal, and Abuses are as familiar to him as it is to be abus'd: We shall therefore leave him a while for his Masters who set him at Work, and distinguish'd him, by giving him the Title of *Secretary to the Confederates* at Will's *Coffee-house*. They may be fine Gentlemen for all that I know in their Chambers, and pretty Conversation for the Ladies they Dress themselves up for; their Coaches may make a noble Appearance, and their Footmens Hatbands may, like their Masters, rise up and take leave of the Crowns of their Hats; their Perukes may be well adjusted, and their Persons set off to the greatest Advantage; yet for all this Sir *R[ichard] Bl[ackmo]re* might chuse whether or no he would be laugh'd at for running into their Commendations. Several of 'em

are Quality by their Cloths, but forfeit the Name by their
Expressions. They have reason perhaps to boast of the *Lady's
Favours*, but will never have any (till they Write better) to
brag of the Reader's. In short, if they are Gentlemen, it's
more than their Verses speak 'em to be; and 'tis manifest,
that they who have chosen *T[om] B[rown]* for their Leader,
fall not a Tittle short of coming up to his admirable Qualifi-
cations. Ev'ry individual Man is a Giant in Scandal, and
shews his Teeth to a Miracle, but what they would have
done, had not the Gentleman they bark'd at been a Physician, it is not in our Power to divine.

Bills, *Pills*, and *Kills* are excellent Rhimes; and they had lost
the greatest part of their *Endeavours* after Satyr, had Sir
Richard been without that Title, which as it has done him
Honour, so he has amply return'd it on the Profession by the
Regularities and Success of his Practice. But we have taken
the liberty to give some Account of their Works, and ought
to do the same by our own; and since in some Places we may
be accus'd for running into the same Faults we blame them
for, we ought to make what Excuses we can for so doing.
We have endeavour'd to answer ev'ry individual Copy as
the Nature of 'em seem'd to require. The Scurrilous we have
return'd a suitable Roughness to, and to the Dull (which
are not very few) a Contempt which is proper for 'em. But
where their Verses have seem'd too long for Epigrams, which
they were design'd for, we have either answer'd 'em with
those that are shorter, or made two or three on the same
Subject; and though the *Covent-Garden* Wits may make
Cuckolds of those Citizens which are *Old* and Superanuated,
yet we hope we have giv'n such a Specimen of our Performance in the following Sheets, that they cannot make *Fools*
of those which are *Young*. And let their Editor be, as soon
as he thinks fit, out with the verses he promis'd us on *Job*
and *Habakkuk*, unless he answers 'em himself, he shall not
stay so long for our Answer as he has been endeavouring at
the performance of his Promise.

In the mean time since his Motto speaks him to be a Reader of *Martial*, without doubt he has met with the following Epigram, which we desire him to apply to himself; and have render'd into English for his Service.

Festive credis te Calliodore jocari,
   Et solum multo permaduisse sale.
Omnibus arrides, dicteria dicis in omnes,
   Sic te Convivam posse placere putas.
At si ego non belle *sed* vere *dixero quiddam,*
   Nemo propinabit Calliodore Tibi.

B[*row*]n Thou believ'st Thou'rt famous for a Jest,
And none like Thou, for Wit, can bear the Test;
Thou flatter'st All, on All Thou fling'st Thy Spight,
Thus think'st Thy Company must needs delight:
But if I speak what's Truth, though course and plain,
Thou ne'er will't have thy Reck'ning *paid* again.

* * *

CV 1 (pp. 1-2)

A Short and True History of the Author of the
Satyr against Wit

[Christopher Codrington]

BY NATURE meant, by Want a Pedant made,
  Bl[*ackmo*]re at first profess'd the Whipping Trade;
Grown fond of Buttocks, he wou'd Lash no more,
But kindly Cur'd the A—— he Gall'd before.
So Quack commenc'd; then, fierce with Pride, he swore,
That Tooth-ach, Gripes, and Corns shou'd be no more.
In vain his Druggs as well as Birch he try'd,
His Boys grew Blockheads, and his Patients dy'd.
Next he turn'd Bard, and, mounted on a Cart,[8]

---

[8] His coach, in which he wrote many of his verses.

Whose hideous Rumbling made *Apollo* start,
Burlesqu'd the Bravest, Wisest Son of *Mars*[9]
In Ballad-rhimes, and all the Pomp of Farce.
Still he chang'd Callings, and at length has hit
On Bus'ness for his matchless Talent fit,
To give us Drenches for the Plague of Wit.[10]

DV 1 (pp. 1-3)

A Short and true History of a certain Captain-General.

By Nature Small, and of a Dwarfish Breed,
Peevish was sent to School, to Write and Read;
Where brib'd by Gifts the Pedagogick Don
Abus'd the Father, and Deceiv'd the Son; [11]
As for a fresh Reward he prais'd his Child,
H'd grasp'd one's Sugar, as he t'other spoil'd.
Thence, swol'n with Figures, and possess'd with Tropes
On *Isis* he bestow'd his Parents Hopes; [12]
And there H'had scarce put on the Tufted-Gown,
And wildly view'd the Colleges and Town,
But Fortune, who no time would let him lose,
Gave him a Royal Infant for his Muse;
And Him he sung with Whimsies in his Brains,
Praising a borrow'd Prince, with borrow'd Strains.[13]

---

[9] King William (or King Arthur).

[10] That neither Sick nor Poore you may neglect,
  For all the Muses *Invalids* erect,
  An Hospital upon *Parnassus* Hill,
  And settle Doctors there of Worth and Skill.
       (*Satyr against Wit*, p. 15)

[11] Codrington attended Dr. Wedale's private school at Enfield. Contrary to the poet's assertion here, Codrington was apparently slender, but tall (Harlow. *Christopher Codrington*, pp. 41-42).

[12] At Oxford, Codrington was one of the leaders of the Christ Church Wits

[13] In 1688 Codrington wrote "In Natalem Sereniss: Principis Walliae" on the birth of the Pretender (see Harlow, pp. 46-47, 221-225).

Next, when the Doubtful Times were chang'd He saw
He left the *Son*, to praise the *Son in Law*;[14]
And with his Righteous Undertaking warm'd,
He star'd, and in Pindarick Frenzie storm'd;
As wisely He the strongest side caress'd,
And *Curs'd* the Babe his selfish Lays had *Bless'd*.
All Matters fix'd, and likely to remain
In favour of the Great *Nassovian's* Reign,
The Dapper 'Squire revolving in his Thought,
That he that Rhim'd, not pleas'd as he that Fought;
To Arms, as fast as Legs would carry, ran,
And Fretfully resolv'd to be a Man.
And since no Spark had walk'd up *High-street* bolder,
The Fellow-Commoner turn'd Fellow-Soldier;
In Camps pursuing what in Schools h'had read,
As he *Lampoon'd* the very Foes he *Fled*.

But Heav'n, least some mischievous Ball should hit
This little Prodigy of Rhimes and Wit,
Put it in *William's* thoughtful Head to make
A *Peace*,[15] and fight no more for Fighting's sake;
Thence he return'd, and a rich Father Dead,
Fatten'd the growing Maggots in his Head,
As he wrote Epigrams for Ladies Smiles,
And govern'd in *B[ow]street* the Leeward Isles.[16]

And now he rides a Tiptoe in his Coach,
Frowning at every Hack that dares approach;
As he by Prince and Subject both prefer'd,

---

[14] When James fled England, Codrington became a staunch supporter of William III.

[15] The Treaty of Ryswick, 1697.

[16] Codrington's father died on July 20, 1698, and the following year Codrington was made Governor-General of the Leeward Islands. For two years he remained in London, settling his personal affairs and concerning himself with the duties of his new position. During this time he took an active part in *Commendatory Verses*, wrote two epilogues (for Dennis and for Southerne), and was a leader of the Wits' circle (Harlow, *Christopher Codrington*, pp. 90-99).

Is own'd a Patron, and adjudg'd a Bard;
A Patron fit for *Br*[*ow*]*n's* and *Ma*[*nnin*]*g's*
    Flights,[17]
If he *Rewards* no better than he *Writes.*

*   *   *

CV 2 (p. 2)

Upon the Author of the Satyr against Wit

[Sir Charles Sedley]

A Grave Physician, us'd to write for Fees,
And Spoil no Paper, but with Recipe's,
Is now turn'd Poet, rails against all Wit,
Except that Little found among the Great.[18]
As if he thought true Wit and Sence were ty'd
To Men in Place, like Avarice, or Pride.
But in their Praise so like a Quack he talks,
You'd swear he wanted for his *Christmas*-box.
With mangled Names old Stories he pollutes,
And to the present Time past Action suits;
Amaz'd we find, in ev'ry Page he writes,
Members of Parliament with *Arthur's* Knights.[19]
It is a common Pastime to write Ill;
And Doctor, with the rest e'en take thy fill.
Thy Satyr's harmless: 'Tis thy Prose that kills,
When thou Prescrib'st thy Potions, and thy Pills.

---

[17] For Brown's relations with Codrington see above, pp. 38-39; Manning dedicated his *Generous Choice* to that patron (see below, p. 140).

[18] Throughout the *Satyr against Wit* especially Blackmore makes a bid for the approval of men of high station, even though some, Sheffield for instance, belong to the Wits circle.

[19] The political allegory in the Arthurian epics is built around a thinly disguised flattery of King William and his court. See above, p. 56.

DV 2 (p. 3)

To the Poetical Knight, *who would have no Body*
spoil Paper but Himself.

A Pox on Rhimes and Physick, S[*ed*]*l*[*e*]*y* cry'd,
(And he had Sense and Reason on his side;)
For both of Rhimes and Physick H'had his fill,
And swallow'd more than ev'ry Verse a Pill.
A Doctor coming by, and loath to lose
A Knight so Famous for a P—— and Muse,
Offer'd him means to give his Knighthood ease,
And make the radicated Torments cease.
Vile Quack, said he, go patch up *Mother Q*[*uar*]*les*,
Sir *Richard* turn Prescriber to Sir *Ch*[*ar*]*l*[*e*]*s*?
It shall not be, jog Homeward if you please,
I'll have no Paper spoil'd on my Disease.
The Doctor cry'd, 'Tis true, th'Infection's such,
Twill certainly discolour't with a Touch;
But I'll affirm, and so withdrawing smil'd,
My Papers may, but Thou can'st ne'er be *Spoil'd.*

*   *   *

CV 3 (pp. 2-3)

To that Incomparable Panegyrist, the Author of the
Satyr upon Wit

[Col. Henry Blount]

Henceforth no more in thy Poetick Rage
Burlesque the God-like Heroes of the Age;
No more King *Arthurs* be with Labour writ,
But follow Nature, and still rail at Wit.
For this thy mighty Genius was design'd,
In this thy Cares a due Success may find.
Opinions we more easily receive
From Guides that practice by those Rules they give:
So Dullness thou may'st write into Esteem,

Thy great Example, as it is thy Theme.
Hope not to joyn, (like G[a]rth's Immortal Lays,)
The keenest Satyr with the finest Praise.
Thy Satyrs bite not, but like *Æsop*'s Ass
Thou kick'st the Darling whom thou would'st caress.
Would'st thou our Youth from Poetry affright,
'Tis wisely done, thy self in Verse to write?
So drunken Slaves the *Spartans* did design
Should fright their Children from the Love of Wine.
Go on, and rail as thou hast done before,
Thus Lovers use when piqu'd in an Amour:
The Nymph they can't enjoy, they call a Whore.

DV 3 (pp. 3-4)

To the Prosaick POET, *occasion'd by the two following Lines*:

Thy Satyrs Bite not, but like Æsop's *Ass,*
Thou Kick'st the Darling whom thou would'st Caress.

'Tis plain that Wit at *Will*'s is very scarce,
By the poor Contradictions of thy Verse;
Else surely some Acquaintance would have made
Those Hobbling Lines speak Sense, which Sense upbraid;
But thou brim full of emptiness of Thought,
Betray'st thy self, and by thy self art caught:
As thou art fashion'd for a standing Jest,
And giv'st us the Reverse of *Æsop*'s Beast;
Who should, if *Bl[ack]more*'s Folly thou'dst have shown,
Caress the Man he'd *Kick*, as Thou hast done.

* * *

CV 4 (p. 3)

The Quack Corrected: or, Advice to the Knight
of the Ill-favour'd Muse.

[Charles Boyle]

Let *Bl*[*ackmo*]*re* still, in good King *Arthur*'s Vein,
To *Fleckno*'s Empire his just Right maintain.
Let him his own to common Sence oppose,
With Praise and Slander maul both Friends and Foes:
Let him great *Dr*[*y*]*d*[*e*]*n*'s awful Name profane;
And learned *G*[*a*]*rth* with envious Pride disdain.
Codron's bright Genius with vile Punns lampoon,
And run a Muck at all the Wits in Town:
Let the Quack scribble any thing but Bills,
His Satyr Wounds not, but his Physick Kills.

DV 4 (p. 4)

The Noble *Corrected; or Advice to a* Quality
Commentator, *who Writes in Defence of* Greek
Epistles as if he understood '*em.*

Let *B*[*oy*]*le* write on, and still'd a Man of Letters,
Prefer Dull Heavy Authors to their Betters;
Let him His own to *B*[*ent*]*ly*'s Sense oppose,
And knowing little fancy much he knows;
Let *D*[*en*]*nis* in his Commendation strain,
And *Codron* praise him, to be prais'd again:
Let ev'ry Wit, and ev'ry Beau declare
What his bright Genius is, and what They are;
As some commend his Parts, and some his Cloths,
Let him be any thing they please in Prose.

But ye, who seemingly appear his Friends,
And basely flatter him for sordid Ends,
Perswade him to avoid the Muses Hill,

And cease to Wound himself, who'd others Kill.
For it's enough that he in Prose is Brave,
And Butchers many an Author in his Grave,
That against Truth, and *Bently*'s Worth he joyns,
And plays the Tyrant o're a Tyrant's Lines.

* * *

CV 5 (p. 4)

To the Merry Poetaster *at* Sadlers-Hall, *in* Cheapside

[Samuel Garth]

Unweildy Pedant, let thy awkward Muse
With Censures praise, with Flatteries abuse.
To lash and not be felt, in Thee's an Art,
Thou ne're mad'st any, but thy School-boys smart.
Then be advis'd, and scribble not agen,
Thou'rt fashion'd for a Flail and not a Pen.
If *B*[*oy*]*l*[*e*]'s immortal Wit thou woud'st decry,
Pretend 'tis He that writ Thy Poetry.
Thy feeble Satyr ne're can do him wrong,
Thy Poems, and thy Patients live not long.

DV 5 (p. 5)

To the Sorry Poetaster at Will'*s* Coffee-House.

Prithee, dear Scribbling Doctor, why so short?
Rail on if thoud'st have *Bl*[*ackmo*]*re* thank thee for't:
Be permanent in Censure and Dispraise,
And grinning shew thy Teeth ten Thousand ways:
For 'tis acknowledg'd by the Court and Town,
Nothing can make him smile like *M*[*anning?*]'s Frown.
He Patients has, 'tis true, which often Die,
And so, thoud'st vainly say perhaps, have I.
But Quack, 'tis false, thy Self-destroying Pill
Ne're had it in its Pow'r as yet to kill,

And as for Patients which thou *Dead* would'st own,
Thou hast as many *Living*, that is *none*.

* * *

CV 6 (p. 4)

An Equal Match: or, A Drawn Battle.

[Christopher Codrington]

A Monument of Dullness to erect,
B[*entle*]*y* shou'd Write, and *Bl*[*ackmo*]*re* shou'd
    Correct;
Like which no other Piece can e're be wrought,
For Decency of Stile, and Life of Thought.
But that where *B*[*entle*]*y* shall in Judgment sit,
To pare Excrescencies from *Bl*[*ackmo*]*re*'s Wit.

DV 6 (p. 5)

An Equal Match, or the Drawn Battle.

If Bards would have a Shortliv'd Poem writ,
P[*atr?*]*ck* should dictate *Rules*, and *T—mb* Wit;
Like which no Mortal piece can e're be found
With Lines of Constitution so unsound.
But that where *T—mb* shall a *Judge* commence,
To file the Rust of *Wit from P*[*atri?*]*ck*'s Sence.

* * *

CV 7 (pp. 4-5)

To the Mirrour of British Knighthood, the
Worthy Author of the Satyr against Wit;
Occasion'd by the Hemystick, P. 8.
            ——Heav'ns Guard poor A[ddiso]n.[20]

[20] In *G*[*arth*] the Wit the Doctor has undone,
In *S*[*malwoo*]*d* the Divine, Heav'ns guard poor *Addison*.
                    (*Satyr against Wit*, p. 8)

[Richard Steele]

Must I then passive stand! and can I hear
The Man I love, abus'd, and yet forbear?
Yet much I thank thy Favour to my Friend,
'Twas some Remorse thou didst not him commend.
Thou dost not all my Indignation raise,
For I prefer thy Pity to thy Praise;

In vain thou woud'st thy Name, dull Pedant, hide,
There's not a Line but smells of thy *Cheapside*,
If *Caesar*'s Bounty for your Trash you've shar'd,
You're not the first Assassine he has spar'd.
His Mercy, not his Justice, made thee Knight,
Which $P[o]rt[e]r$ [21] may demand with equal Right.

Well may'st thou think an useless Talent Wit,
Thou who without it hast three Poems Writ:
Impenetrably dull, secure thou'rt found,
And can'st receive no more, than give a Wound;
Then, scorn'd by all, to some dark Corner fly,
And in Lethargic Trance expiring lie,
Till thou from injur'd $G[a]rth$ thy Cure receive,
And $S[malwoo]d$ only Absolution give.

DV 7 (p. 6)

To the Noble Captain, *who was in a Damn'd
Confounded Pet, because the Author of the* Satyr
against Wit, *was pleas'd to Pray for his Friend,
occasion'd by this Distich:*

*His Mercy, not his Justice, made thee Knight,
Which* $P[orte]r$ *may demand with equal Right.*

Bold Man of War, the drift of thy Designs?
And let us know the meaning of thy Lines.

---

[21] George Porter was one of the fanatical Jacobites who planned to assassinate William III in 1696. The Plot was revealed by Sir Thomas Prendergast, who stipulated that Porter's life should be spared. Porter was pardoned when he turned King's evidence (*DNB*, XLVI, 176-177).

If Mercy is a Suff'rance of a Fact,
How comes it then to give Rewards, and act?
Define, and tell us when thou'rt in the right,
And own that Mercy spares, but cannot Knight.
P[orte]r and *Thou* may be forgot and spar'd,
He for a Traytor, thou a Senceless Bard.
Yet neither can attone for either's Crimes,
He for his Foolish Plot, or *Thou* for Rhymes.
Though D[ra]ke to purge thy Muse shou'd Physick send,
Or S[malwoo]d should absolve him as a Friend.

* * *

CV 8 (p. 5)

To the Cheapside *Knight, on his* Satyr against Wit,
[William Burnaby or John Dennis?]

Some scribling Fops so little value Fame,
They sometimes hit, because they never Aim.
But thou for Erring, has a certain Rule,
And, aiming, art inviolably Dull.
Thy muddy Stream no lucid Drop supplies,
But Punns like Bubbles on the Surface rise.
All that for Wit you cou'd, you've kindly done,
You cannot write, but can be writ upon.
And a like Fate does either side befit,
Immortal Dullness, or Immortal Wit:
In just Extreams an equal Merit lies,
And B[oy]le and G[a]rth with thee must share the Prize, ⎫
Since thou canst sink, as much as they can rise. ⎭

DV 8 (pp. 6-7)

To the Inviolably Dull Critick, on his Heroical
Strains upon the Satyr against Wit.

Some Scribbling Fops as D[enn]is is by Name, ⎫
Never can hit, although they always aim, ⎬
And Storm, and Swear, and Drink, and Write for Fame. ⎭

What Star prevents 'em, or what Planet shines,
To keep the Lucky Goddess from their Lines;
Let those decide, who have it in their Sphere,
Doubtless they err, because they persevere.
  But thou, my crabbed piece of blustring Wit.
Erring do'st think the wish'd for Mark is hit;
And, Pox upon thy Judgment and thy Skull,
Labour'st to be thought intricate and dull.
For shame, Grave Don, 'tis time that thou wer't wise,
Having seen Years enough before thine Eyes.
E'en do, as Men of Ancient standing shou'd,
Or understand, or else be understood,
Since 'tis in vain to shew thy fruitless spight,
And thou can'st find less Faults, than thou canst write.

* * *

CV 9 (p. 6)

To the Indefatigable Rhimer.

[Dr. Thomas Smith]

O S[ome]rs, T[albo]t, D[ors]ett, M[onta]gue,
G[re]y, S[heffie]ld, C[avendi]sh, P[embro]ke,
V[erno]n,[22] you

---

[22] These opening lines mimic Blackmore's in the *Satyr against Wit* (p. 9):

> O S[om]er, T[albo]t, D[or]set, M[onta]gue,
> Gr[e]y, Sh[effie]ld, C[an]d[i]sh, P[embro]ke,
> V[erno]n, you
> Who in *Parnassus* have Imperial Sway,
> Whom all the Muses Subjects here obey,
> Are in your Service and Receive your Pay;
> Exert your Sovereign Power, in Judgment sit
> To regulate the Nation's Grievance, Wit.

Blackmore's genuflecting was, it should be remembered, in the best tradition of the day, though the Wits made much of it. Blackmore had picked on men

Who suffer *Bl[ackmo]re* to insult your tast,
And tamely hear him bluster in bombast.
Bid him before he dares to write agen,
Resign his own, and take some other Pen.
D[ryde]n, shall Numbers, *C[ongre]ve* Wit inspire,
Dr[a]ke[23] nicest Rules, but *B[oy]le* and *Codron*[24] Fire.
Then *G[a]rth* shall teach him, and his witless Tribe
First to write Sence, and after to Prescribe;
The unlearn'd Pedant, thus may please the Town,
But his own nauseous Trash will ne're go down.
For naught can equal, what the Bard has writ,
But *R[adcli]ff[e]*'s[25] Scholarship, and *G[ibbo]n*'s[26] Wit.

---

of importance: John, Lord Somers, the Lord Chancellor, a well-known patron of the arts and a member of the Kit-Cat club; Charles Talbot, the Earl of Shrewsbury, a secretary of state and a leader of William's party; Charles Sackville, the Earl of Dorset, a poet popular among the Wits and a generous literary patron; Charles Montague, the Earl of Halifax, patron and writer and Chancellor of the Exchequer; Thomas Grey, the Earl of Stamford, and James Vernon held various posts of importance under William; the Earl of Pembroke, Thomas Herbert, lord high admiral and a president of the Royal Society; John Sheffield, the Earl of Mulgrave and Duke of Buckingham, probably wrote one of the poems in *Commendatory Verses* attacking Blackmore (see below, pp. 142-143; William Cavendish (sometimes spelled "Candish"), the Duke of Devonshire, a high official under William.

[23] A strong Dispensarian, Dr. James Drake was also a literary critic of some standing; he entered the Collier controversy with his *Antient and Modern Stages Survey'd* (1699).

[24] Christopher Codrington.

[25] The place of John Radcliffe (frequently spelled "Ratcliffe") in the *Commendatory Verses* quarrel is not clear. A wealthy doctor, from whose benefactions Oxford later profited, Radcliffe was at one time Tom Brown's patron; in the poem prefixed to the *Dispensary*, Codrington spoke respectfully of him as "thoughtful *R[adcliff]e*." On the other hand, Blackmore praised him in the *Satyr against Wit*, once again reflecting the complexity of the controversy. Radcliffe is probably attacked in *Commendatory Verses* 9 (and again in 40, where his Yorkshire brogue is ridiculed) because he failed to support the Dispensary, a project which threatened the fat profits he was sharing with the apothecaries (B. Boyce, *Tom Brown*, p. 60).

[26] Dr. William Gibbons, the Mirmillo of Garth's poem, the *Dispensary*, also supported the apothecaries.

DV 9 (p. 7)

To a Rhimer, *who if he takes pains, Writes as if he did not.*

Who e'er Thou art, to Me and Sense unknown,
Correct not others Follies but thy own;
Nor dare to Censure *R*[*adcli*]*ff*'s healing Arts,
Or point at *G*[*ibbo*]*n*'s Wit thy Leaden Darts.
What have they done to call thy Nonsense forth,
And make thee shew thy Penury of Worth?
Or how could *B*[*lackmo*]*re*'s Muse deserve thy Spight,
Unless it was for teaching thee to write?

Prithee, for shame acknowledge this Offence,
And own 'em Men of Skill, and Men of Sence.
But Oh! Kind Heav'n forbid it that thy Quill
Should dare t'attempt their Judgment or their Skill,
That thou should'st rise and injure 'em with praise,
And stab their Reputations with thy Lays,
For nothing but the poison of thy Lines,
Defeats their Cure, and mocks their great Designs.

*   *   *

CV 10 (p. 6)

A modest Request to the Poetical Knight.

[Christopher Codrington or Anthony Henley?]

Since, *Be*[*ntle*]*y*'s Nonsence to outdo, you strive,
Vain to be thought the Dullest Wretch alive,
And such Inimitable Strains have writ,
That the most famous Blockheads must submit:
Long may you Reign, and long unenvy'd Live,
And none Invade your great Prerogative.
But in Return, your Poetry give o're,
And Persecute poor *Job*, and us no more.

DV 10 (p. 8)

A Modest Request to the Poetical Squire.

Since you to Poetry will make pretence,
And H[en?]ly'll be a Wit in H[en?]ly's Sence,
As you resign'd to Dullness, in your Chair,
Think on foul Lines to gratifie the Fair:
Long may you Rhime, and on your Lute and Spinnet
Play many a woful Tune with nothing in it.

But in return my dear Facetious Squire,
For once to gratifie a Friends desire,
Think as I do, you'll fling your Verses in the Fire.

*   *   *

CV 11 (p. 7)

Wholesome Advice to a City Knight,
    Over-run with Rhimes and Hypocrisie:
    Occasion'd by his Satyr against Wit.

[Earl of Anglesea]

We bid thee not give o're the Killing Trade:
Whilst Fees come in, 'tis fruitless to diswade,
Religion is a Trick, you've practis'd long,
To bring in Pence, and gull the gaping Throng.
But all thy Patients now perceive thy Aim,
They find thy Morals, and thy Skill the same.
Then, if thou would'st thy Ignorance redress,
Prythee mind Physick more, and Rhiming less.

DV 11 (p. 8)

To a L[or]d who would be a Saint, if he was as free
    from all other Sins, as he is from Hypocrisie.

Advice to P[ee]rs, th' Adviser's Zeal may prove,
But ne're like Praise can swell 'em into Love.

Then give me leave to do the thing that's safe,
And fling away some Verse in your Behalf.

That you have Travell'd, is exceeding true,
And that your L[ordshi]p's Muse hath Teeth to shew,
But among all the Frolicks you have shewn,
Religion is a *Trick* you ne'er have known.

* * *

CV 12   (pp. 7-8)

To a thrice Illustrious Quack, Pedant, and Bard, on his
Incomparable Poem call'd, A Satyr against Wit.

By a Lady [the Countess of Sandwich]

Thou fund of Nonsence, was it not enough
That Cits and pious Ladies lik'd thy Stuff,
That as thou Copy'dst *Virgil*,[27] all might see
Judicious Bell-men Imitated thee.
That to thy Cadence Sextons set their Chimes,
And Nurses skimming Possets hum'd thy Rhimes.
But thou must needs fall foul on Men of Sence,
With Dullness equal to thy Impudence.
Are D[ryde]n, C[o]dr[ingto]n, G[ar]th, V[anbroo]k,
    B[oy]le,
Those Names of Wonder, that adorn our Isle,
Fit Subjects for thy vile Pedantick Pen?
Hence sawcy Usher to thy Desk again:
Construe Dutch Notes, and pore upon Boys A——es,
But prithee write no more Heroick Farces.
Teach blooming Blockheads by thy own try'd Rules
To give us Demonstration that they're Fools.
Let 'em by *N*——'s Sermon-stile refine
Their English Prose, their Poetry by thine.

---

[27] Blackmore borrowed extensively from Virgil. See Roberta F. Brinkley,
Arthurian Legend in the Seventeenth Century (see p. 16, n. 17) pp. 149-151.

Let $W[e]sl[e]y$'s [28] Rhimes their Emulation raise,
And $Arw[a]k[e]r$,[29] Instruct 'em how to Praise.
That, when all Ages in this Truth agree,
They're finished Dunces, they may rival thee,
Thou only Stain to Mighty WILLIAM's Sword!
Old *Jemmy* [30] never Knighted such a *T——d*.
For the most nauseous Mixture GOD can make,
Is a dull Pedant, and a busy Quack.

DV 12 (pp. 8-9)

To a Lady dignified and distinguish'd by the Name
of Critick *and* Poet, *on Her incomprehensible*
Raileries on the Satyr against Wit.

Believe me, Madam, that your Muse has shown
So foul a Face, I beg you hide your own;
And if you'r real Quality be Civil,
For T——d and A——se all over is the Devil.

That you're no Pious Lady is confess'd,
By making *Wesly*'s Sacred Work your Jest;
Which (tho' it does not with the Witty take)
Might please the Wise for its great Subjects sake.
Not but I think you've been at Church sometimes,
Because you write of Sextons and of Chimes;
But that you are a Woman few can tell
So right, as those you think you praise so well.

---

[28] Samuel Wesley, the father of John and Charles, founders of Methodism. In such works as his *Maggots: or Poems on Several Subjects, never before Handled. By a Schollar* (1685) he won the contempt of the Wits, who jeered at his " Holy Dogrel " (*Compleat Key to the Seventh Edition of the Dispensary,* 1716, p. 19). He made the further mistake of praising Blackmore's poetry. Pope pilloried Wesley in the first edition of the *Dunciad* (1728, I, 115).

[29] Edmund Arwaker wrote about a dozen fulsome poems celebrating famous people. Such pieces as his *Poem Humbly Delicated to the Queen. On the Occasion of her Majestys Happy Conception* (1688) aroused the Wits' mirth.

[30] King James.

For Heaven's sake, Madam, qualifie this Fit,
Some speak you Nobly Born, and yet a Wit?
Nor let me be successless in my Pray'r,
A Muse should not take up a Lady's care;
For 'tis a Composition most absurd,
That's made of Rhimes, of Woman, and of Turd.

* * *

CV 13 (p. 8)

To Sir R[ichard] Bl[ackmo]re, *on the Report of
the Two* ARTHURS *being condemn'd to be hang'd.*

Once more take Pen in Hand, Obsequious Knight,
For here's a Theme thou canst not underwrite,
Unless the Devil ow's thy Muse a Spite.
To Prince and King thy Dullness Life did give,
Let then these *Arthurs* too in Dogg'rel live.

DV 13 (p. 9)

To an Author, *who never wrote but two Distichs
and an half, and those could not pass Muster.*

You bid me take my Pen again, 'tis true,
But I shall scarce request the same of You.
Five Lines already have your Judgment shewn,
Tho' you'd be more esteem'd for writing none;
And if excess of *Dulness Life can give,*
You need not scribble Knight, you'r sure to *Live.*

* * *

CV 14 (pp. 8-9)

Occasion'd by the News that Sir R[ichard]
Bl[ackmore]'s *Paraphrase upon* Job *was in
the Press.*

[Tom Brown]

When *Job,* contending with the Devil, I saw,
It did my Wonder, but not Pity draw:

For I concluded, that without some Trick,
A Saint at any time cou'd match Old Nick.

Next came a fiercer Fiend upon his Back,
I mean his Spouse, and stunn'd him with her Clack.
But still I cou'd not pity him, as knowing
A Crabtree-cudgel soon wou'd send her going.

But when the *Quack* engag'd with *Job* I spy'd,
The Lord have Mercy on poor *Job*, I cry'd.
What *Spouse* and *Satan* did attempt in vain,
The *Quack* will compass with his murdring Pen,
And on a Dunghil leave poor *Job* again,
With impious Dogg'rel he'll pollute his Theme,
And make the Saint against his Will Blaspheme.

DV 14 (p. 10)

Occasion'd by the News that Tom B[row]n *had the
Courage to Engage with Sir* Richard Blackmore,
after his Bookseller *had Defeated him.*[31]

When B[rown] Contending I with R[ope]r spy'd,
I wonder'd, but not pitty'd either side;
Well knowing, if they were of Scratching sick,
Abel could buy, and *Tom* could beg a Stick.

Next came a Dun, and at his Garret stood,
He'd have his Money truly that he wou'd;
But still I could not pity him, as knowing
Tom would soon find a Trick to send him going.

But when I saw him brandishing his Muse,
The Bad to Flatter, and the Good Abuse,
With Pity then, and much Concern, I cry'd,
Tom, Do'st thou know what Folly's on thy side?

---

[31] For the story of Brown's quarrel with Roper see above, p. 38, n. 3.

Give the fierce waspish Col'nel back his Gold,
Nor let thy Praise be bought, thy Lies be sold;
Blackmore and *Job* (believe it) will subdue
Ten Thousand such Malicious Fiends as You.

How? Said the Bard, Most excellent Advice!
A Poet, and be Master of a Sice? [32]
Find out that Place where e're I paid one Score,
Then I'll return the Guinea's, not before.

* * *

CV 15 (pp. 9-10)

A TALE.

[Christopher Codrington]

Poems and Prose of different Force lay Claim
With the same Confidence to *Tully's* Name.
And shallow Criticks were content to say,
Prose was his Bus'ness, Poetry his Play.
Thus *Caesar* thought, thus *Brutus* and the rest,
Who knew the Man, and knew his Talent best.

Maurus [33] arose; sworn Foe to Health and Wit,
Who *Folio* Bills and *Folio* Ballads writ.
Who bustled much for Bread, and for Renown,
By Lyes and Poison scatter'd through the Town.
To *Roman* Wives with Veneration known,
For *Roman* Wives were very like our own.
And Husbands then we find in *Latin* Song
Wou'd Love too little, and wou'd Live too long.
Tully, says he, 'tis plain to Friends and Foes,
Writes his own Verse, but borrows all his Prose.
He Fearless was, because he was not Brave,

---

[32] Slang for " sixpence," *NED* (IX, pt. 1, p. 4).   [33] Blackmore.

A Noble *Roman* wou'd not beat a Slave.
The *Consul* smiling, said, Judicious Friend,
Thy shining Genius shall thy Works defend.
Inimitable Stroaks defend thy Fame,
Thy Beauties and thy Force are still the same.
And I must yield with the consenting Town,
Thy Ballads, and thy Bills, are all thy own.

DV 15 (pp. 10-11)

A Tale taken to pieces.

If *Shallow Criticks*, as your pleas'd to say,
Judge *Tully* when at *Poetry* at *Play*,
And Ignorance would censure and suppose
He ne'er had been a *Consul* but for Prose:
How comes it then that *Caesar*, who's confess'd
To know the Man, and know his Talent best,
Who in Fame's List for Judgment is enroll'd,
(Whether you mean the Modern or the Old)
Should with the *Shallow* for a *Judge* be brought,
And make their Sence authentick with his Thought.

O Youth, tho' sweet and flowing be thy Song,
Thy Numbers beautious, and thy Beauties strong;
Tho' *Force* and *Ease* alternately appear,
And Fancy glads the Sight, and charms the Ear;
Yet, if amidst thy Turns of *Verse* and *Thought*
Mistake should blend, or Hast neglect a Fault;
If uncorrected Errors shall be found
T'offend our Senses, or our Judgments wound;
As to be *fearless*, is not to be *Brave*,
And *Squire's* a *Noble*, while a *Knight's* a Slave;
In vain you measure out your fruitless Lays,
And gloss your want of Sence with gilded Praise;
For if you'd write with Credit and Success,
You must mind *Judgment* more, and *Friendship* less.

* * *

CV 16 (pp. 10-11)

Upon the Character of Codron,[34] *as 'tis drawn by
the Bungling Knight in his* Satyr against Wit.

[William Walsh]

How kind is Malice manag'd by a Sot,
Where no Design directs the *Embrio* Thought,
And Praise and Satyr stumble out by Lot.
The Mortal Thrust to *Codron*'s Heart design'd,
Proves a soft wanton Touch to charm his Mind.
Can *M*[*o*]*nt*[*a*]*gue* or *D*[*o*]*rs*[*e*]*t* higher soar!
Or can Immortal *Sh*[*e*]*ff*[*ie*]*ld* wish for more?
Brightness, Force, Justness, Delicacy, Ease,
Must form that Wit, that can the Ladies please.
No false affected Rules debauch their Taste,
No fruitless Toils their generous Spirits wast,
Which wear a Wit into a Dunce at last.
No lumber-Learning gives an awkward Pride,
False Maxims cramp not, nor false Lights misguide.
Voiture and *W*[*a*]*lsh* [35] their easie Hours employ,
Voiture and *W*[*a*]*lsh* oft read will never cloy.
With Care they guard the Musick of their Style,
They fly from *B*[*ent*]*l*[*e*]*y*, and converse with *B*[*oy*]*le*.
They steal no Terms, no Notions from the Schools,
The Pedant's Pleasure, and the Pride of Fools;
With native Charms their matchless Thoughts surprize,
Soft as their Souls, and beauteous as their Eyes.
Gay as the Light, and unconfin'd as Air,
Chaste and Sublime, all worthy of the Fair.
How then can a rough artless *Indian* Wit [36]

---

[34] Codrington.

[35] Vincent Voiture was in vogue in England at the time. His letters were
translated by Tom Brown, and by Dryden, Dennis, and Thomas Cheek in 1700
(*Familiar and Courtly Letters, Written by Monsieur Voiture;* reissued in 1701,
1704, 1705).

[36] West Indian. Codrington was appointed governor of the Leeward Islands
in 1699.

The faultless Palates of the Ladies fit?
Codron will never stand so nice a Test,
Nor is't with Praise fair Mouths oblige him best.
Let others make a vain Parade of Parts,
Whilst *Codron* aims not at Applause, but Hearts.
Secure him those, and thou shall't name the rest,
Thy Spite shall choose the worst, thy Taste the best.
He will his Health to *Mirmil's* [37] Care resign,
He will with *Buxtorf* and with *B[ent]ly* shine,
And be a Wit in any way, but thine.

DV 16 (p. 11)

To Codron*'s and the* Lady's *Humble Servant.*

Not that I blame your Flatt'ry, or your Spleen,
But prithee give's the Sense of what you mean:
Can *Bl[ackmo]re* write without *Design*, or Art,
And yet *design* a —— at *Codron's* Heart?
Unthinking Bard! stuff'd up with Praise and Spight,
Gravely consider next before you write;
And if you'd shew a Man of Sense and Stile,
Bring other Vouchers than a Lady's Smile:
For if I know 'em well, they'd rather chuse
His *P[es]tle* to *divert* 'em than his *Muse.*

DV 17 (p. 12)

To the same, on the same Subject.

C O D R O N may *please* the *Ladies*, as he writes,
And pretty things for pretty things Endites;
But Thou be damn'd, and fling away thy Pen,
Such *Fops* as Thou, can never *please* the *Men.*

---

[37] Dr. William Gibbons, an anti-Dispensarian, was attacked under the name of " Mirmillo " by Garth in the *Dispensary.*

DV 18 (p. 12)

*To the same, occasion'd by the Verse which reflects
on Dr.* Gibbons, (viz.)

He will his Health to Mirmil'*s Care resign.*

Friend, by my Soul, the Devil's in thy Quill,
Or Thou would'st never write and judge so ill;
For whilst thou Laugh'st at *Gibbon*'s skill, 'tis sure,
Thou stand'st in need thy self of **Tyson*'s Cure.
Nor would the Youth, the Subject of thy Song,
Accept thy Flatt'ries, or permit thy Tongue
To blast his Credit with defaming Praise,
And take Lethargick *Opiats* from thy *Lays*;
Was *He* the *Man* thy Rhimes would have him be,
Or *Thou* the *Man* for whom he judges thee.

*   *   *

CV 17 (p. 11)

An Epigram on Job *Travesty'd by the* City Bard.

[Christopher Codrington or Knightly Chetwood?]

Poor *Job* lost all the Comforts of his Life,
And hardly sav'd a Potsherd, and a Wife.
Yet *Job* blest God, and Job again was blest,
His Vertue was Essay'd, and bore the Test.
But had Heav'n's Wrath pour'd out its fiercest Vial, ⎫
Had he been then Burlesqu'd, without denial ⎬
The patient Man had yielded to that Trial. ⎭
His pious Spouse with *Bl[ackmo]re* on her side
Must have prevail'd, and *Job* had curst, and dy'd.

DV 19 (p. 12)

An Epigram on Dr. Ch[etw]ood.

Poor *Job* was *plagu'd*, of Holy *Men* the best,
But *Ch[etw]ood sins*, and in this Life is *Bless'd*;

---

* *Dr.* Tyson *is Physitian to* Bethlem *Hospital.* (Original note.)

With Losses he, and Pains, and Fire was vex'd,
And he *divides Fat Capons* with his Text.
One had a *Fiend* and Woman to perswade,
But t'other He can *Curse* without their *aid*.
As he delights to play the *Tempter's* part,
And labours to be Damn'd with all his Heart.
When having lost the *Preacher* in the *Beast*,
He shews the *Devil*, who should act the *Priest*.

* * *

CV 18 (pp. 11-12)

To the Adventurous Knight of Cheapside, *upon his*
Satyr against Wit.

[Francis Manning?]

What Frenzy has possess'd thy desp'rate Brain,
To Rail at Wit in this unhallow'd Strain?
Reproach of thy own Kind! to slander Sense,
The noblest Gift bestow'd by Providence!
Was it Revenge provok'd thee thus to Write,
Because thou'rt curs'd to such a Dearth of Wit?
Or was it eager Passion for a Name,
To be inroll'd among the Fools of Fame?
Like him, who rather than he'd live obscure,
Would Fire a Church to make his Name secure.
Or was it thy Despair at length to find
Thy Loads of Chaff the Sport of every Wind?
To see thy hasty Muse, that loves to roam,
Promise such Journies, but come founder'd home?
Just Fate of Sots, who think in their vain Breast,
Their Coffee-Rhimes shall stand the Publick Test:
Seiz'd with prolifick Dullness, 'tis thy Curse,
To Write still on, and still too for the Worse.
Who hates not *Wes*[*le*]*y*, may Thy Works esteem,
Both alike able to Disgrace their Theme.
But Thou, thro' wild Conceit aspiring still,

Claim'st in Thy Ravings *Esculapian*-skill.
Quack thou art sure in Both, and curs'd is he,
Who guided by his adverse Stars to Thee,
Employs thy deadly Potions to reclaim
His feeble Health, thy Pen to spread his Fame.

DV 20 (p. 13)

An Answer to a great many Impertinent Questions.

Methinks you take too much upon you, Sir,
And tho' you stirring stink, you needs must stir;
Else, why so many Foolish Queries brought
T'upbraid the Querist's want of Sence and Thought?
That he found fault with Wit, is very true,
But, Captain, what a Pox is that to you?
Untouch'd by Satyr you may safely pass,
Unless to be a Wit's to be an A——.

DV 21 (p. 13)

To the same upon his calling Sir R[ichard] B[lackmo]re's
Composures, Coffee Rhimes.

If Coffee does Awake the Senses keep,
And guards our Eye-lids from approaching Sleep,
Well hast thou giv'n the Doctor's Rhimes the Name,
And prais'd his Merits, which thou would'st defame;
For we with *wakeful* Pleasure can peruse,
And meditate the Beauties of his Muse,
When *Thy* Composures we for *Opiats* take,
And only run 'em o're for *Sleepings* sake.

* * *

CV 19 (p. 12)

*Upon the Knighting of Sir R—— BL——RE, for his
Incomparable Poem call'd,* King *A R T H U R.*

[Tom Brown]

Be not puff'd up with Knighthood, Friend of mine,
A merry Prince once Knighted a Sir-Loyn.[38]
And, if to make Comparisons 'twere safe,
An *Ox* deserv'd it better than a *Calf.*
Thy Pride and State I value not a Rush,
Thou that art now King *Phyz,* wast once King Ush.[39]

DV 22 (p. 13)

To the Quibling, *Drib'ling, Scribling* Poetaster, *who
has let himself out for Scandal to the Wits at
Will's* Coffee-House.

Be not puff'd up with Punning, Friend of mine,
I've Slept o'er many Jests as good as thine;
And tho' at present thou may'st strut and stare,
Blown up with *Treats* and *Covent-Garden* Air;
Yet when their Turns are serv'd, believe it, then
Spark thou must *Dine* on Smoak at *How's*[40] again;
So different is thy wretched State from his,
Thou *hast* been *Ush,* but never can'st be *Phiz.*

*   *   *

[38] According to popular etymology. Thomas Fuller is sometimes quoted in
this connection (*Church History of Britain,* VI, ii, 299): " A Sir-loyne of beef
was set before Him (so knighted, saith tradition, by this King Henry [the
Eighth])." The story is also told about James I and Charles II (*NED, IX,* i,
103).

[39] *Alluding to the two Kings in the* Rehearsal. (Original note.) [Written
by George Villiers, Duke of Buckingham, and others, the *Rehearsal* (1671)
burlesqued the popular heroic tragedies of the Restoration. The King Physician
and the King Usher, who usurp the throne from the two Kings of Brentford,
are equally ludicrous. Tom Brown is simply saying here that Blackmore is just
as ridiculous now as he was before he was knighted.]

[40] A coffee house.

CV 20 (p. 13)

Upon King ARTHUR, *partly written in the Doctor's Coach, and partly in a Coffee-house.*

[Tom Brown]

Let the malicious Criticks Snarl and Rail,
Arthur immortal is, and must prevail.
In vain they strive to wound him with their Tongue,
The Lifeless *Fœtus* can receive no wrong.
As rattling Coach once thunder'd through the Mire,
Out dropt Abortive *Arthur* from his Sire.[41]
Well may he then both Time and Death defie,
For what was never born, can never die.

DV 23 (p. 14)

To the same Trifling Fellow, T[om] B[row]n.

Dame Fortune's just, malicious Fool, I see
By what sh' has done for *Blackmore*, and for thee.
He in his Chariot, which is paid for, sits,
And dares the feeble Spleen of Thredbare Wits,
Who just like thou brush'd out in Tally Suit,
Laugh at his *Coach*, but Rascals, laugh a *foot*.
E'en take thy fill, and play a *Zany*'s part,
And censure Judgment, and reflect on Art,
While he by Parents, and by Children bless'd,
By Husbands pray'd for, and by Wives caress'd,
Brings Health and Safety at the Patient's call,
And *rises* when thou can'st not lower *fall*.

* * *

---

[41] A reference to Blackmore's admitted habit of composing verses in his coach while making professional calls.

CV 21 (p. 13)

Upon seeing a Man light a Pipe of Tobacco in
a Coffee-house, with a Leaf of King ARTHUR.

[Tom Brown]

In Coffee-house begot,[42] the short-liv'd Brat,
By instinct thither hasts to meet his Fate.
The *Phœnix* to *Arabia* thus returns,
And in the Grove, that gave her Birth, she burns.
Thus wandring *Scot*, when through the World he's past, ⎫
Revisits ancient *Tweed* with pious haste,   ⎬
And on Paternal Mountain dies at last.   ⎭

DV 24 (p. 14)

Upon seeing a Man wipe his A—se *with* T[om] B[rown]'s
Satyr *against the* French King.

If shitten *Lines* should wipe a shitten *A—se*,
Thomas, the Man does Justice to thy Verse;
As it was *Born*, whatever thou may'st think,
Thy *Ballad* makes its *Exit* too in *Stink*.
When Mortal Man is buried, then the Word
Is *Dust to Dust*, but here it's *T—d* to *T—d*.

* * *

CV 22 (p. 14)

EPIGRAM,

Occasion'd by the Passage in the Satyr against Wit,
that Reflects upon Mr. Tate, *and ends thus,*

He's Honest, and, as Wit comes in, will Pay.[43]

[Tom Brown or Nicholas Brady?]

Rail on, discourteous Knight. If modest *Tate*
Is slow in making Payments, what of that!

---

[42] Blackmore is supposed to have written some of his verses in coffee houses.
[43] *T*[*at*]*e* will subscribe, but set no Payment-Day,
For his slow Muse you must with Patience stay,
He's honest, and as Wit comes in, will pay.
(*Satyr against Wit*, p. 11.)

So is th' Exchequer, so are half the Lords,
On whom thou hast bestow'd such Sugar'd Words.
Envy itself must own this Truth of *Nahum*,*
That when the Muses call, he strives to pay 'em.
But can we this of thy damn'd Hackney say,
Who as she nothing has, can nothing pay?
Then be advis'd; Rail not at *Tate* so fast,
A Psalm of his may chance to be thy last.[44]

DV 25 (p. 14)

An Epigram, occasion'd by Mr. B[ra]dy*'s, about
his Friend Mr.* Tate.

Prithee, my gentle Man of Crape, and Pray'r,
Why so concern'd, and full of Noise and Care?
T[*at*]*e*, 'tis allow'd, makes Payments when he can,
And slowly shews himself an Honest Man:
But I ne'er heard of *B*[*ra*]*dy*'s *Payments* yet,
Either in ready *Money*, or in *Wit*.
Then rest contented, as a Man should be,
Sir *Richard* ne'er will say the *same* of *Thee*.

* * *

CV 23 (p. 14)

A Story of a Greek *Chevalier, Predecessor in a
direct Line to the* British *Knight.*

[Tom Brown or John Sheffield?]

When, fir'd by Glory, *Philip*'s Godlike Son,
The *Persian* Empire like a Storm o'rerun,
A worthless Scribbler, *Chœrilus*[45] by Name,

---

* *Mr.* Tate's *Christian Name.* (Original note.)

[44] Tate and Nicholas Brady had just put out a new version of the Psalms (see below, pp. 134-135).

[45] According to their bargain, Alexander was to give the poet a blow for every bad line he wrote, and a gold piece for every good one. This information is contained in Acron's scholium on Horace, *Ars Poetica*, 357. Acron adds that the blows were so numerous as to cause the poet's death.

In pompous Dogg'rel soil'd the Hero's Fame.
The *Grecian* Prince, to Merit ever just,
(For Monarchs did not then Reward on Trust)
Read o're his Rhimes, and to chastise such Trash,
Gave him for each offending Line a Lash.
Thus Bard went off, with many Drubs requited,
That's in plain English, *Chœrilus* was Knighted.

DV 26 (p. 15)

A Reply to the Story of the Greek Chevalier.

If Monarch's (as you'll hav't) on Trust reward,
I shall not ask why *Sh[effie]ld* was prefer'd?
But I'll be sworn, and vouch, it as 'tis true,
That Author's baulk'd, who waits Rewards from you.

DV 27 (p. 15)

To the same.

If you'r a *L[or]d,* as whispering Fame reports,
And know the Constitutions well of courts,
Does not your Honour think 'twould be a hard case,
He could not make a Knight, who made a M[arqui]ss.

* * *

CV 24 (p. 15)

To the Pious and Worthy Author of the Satyr
against Wit.

Bl[ackmo]re strove long with holy Crafts to please,
Some thought him serious, therefore gave him Fees;
Much Sanctity before his Books He shows,
But, whom his Preface gains, his Poems lose.
No Patients now consult him; thus we find
His Practice with his Poetry's declin'd.

DV 28 (p. 15)

To the Unworthy Author of the Verses on the Satyr against Wit.

If *B*[*lackmo*]*re* labours as he writes, to please,
Why do'st not thou consult thy Reader's Ease?
And hammer out a Thought may shew thy pains,
To countenance thy Scarcity of Brains?
Sence may decline, and Wit consummate may
Wear itself out in time, and know decay;
But Wit like thine, and stumbling into Rhime,
Defies the Injuries of Fate, or Time:
'Tis still the same amongst the Learn'd and Wise,
And as it cannot *fall*, it cannot *rise*.

* * *

CV 25 (pp. 15-16)

Melancholy Reflections on the Deficiency of Useful Learning

To Sir R[ichard] Bl[ackmo]re.

[Dr. Edward Baynard?]

Short are our Powers, tho' infinite our Will:
What Helps to useful Knowledge want we still!
Laborious *L*[*i*]*st*[*e*]*r* [46] thirty Years employs
In painful search of Nature's curious Toys:
Yet many a painted Shell, and shining Fly
Must still in Dirt, and dark Oblivion lye.
Mysterious *Sl*[*oa*]*ne* [47] may yet go on to stun ye

---

[46] An eminent doctor, Martin Lister was also a zoologist, natural historian, and an authority on Yorkshire antiquities. He was the author of forty pieces in the *Philosophical Transactions* of the Royal Society, of which he was a Fellow.

[47] Sir Hans Sloane, physician, botanist, was responsible for reviving the *Philosophical Transactions* of the Royal Society, which had been suspended; he supervised their publication until 1712. His natural history collections helped lay the foundation for the British Museum. Since both Lister and Sloane were in favor of the Dispensary, it is difficult to see why they are ridiculed here, unless

With *Cynocrambe, Poppy-pye, Bumbunny*;
But from what Records can we hope to know
If poor *Will. *Matthew*'s Babes surviv'd or no?
Æras from costly Mummeries arose,
But who th' important Moment shall disclose
'Till *B*[*e*]*ntl*[*e*]*y* writes of *Grecian* Puppet-shows?
Heralds are paid, and Registers are kept
Of ancient Knights, who in full Glory slept.
But *Garter* nods; *Garter* assigns no Place
To three illustrious Knights of *English* Race:
Nor will succeeding *Britains* hear one Word
Of good Sir-*Loin*, Sir *Richard*, or Sir *T*——.

DV 29 (p. 15)

Merry Thoughts on Dr. B[aynar]d*'s Melancholy
Reflections on the Deficiency of* Useful Learning.

That *B*[*aynar*]*d* Raves, both Friends and Foes
  conclude,
Yet neither Friends nor Foes can say he's rude;
Rudeness they know's a meditated Crime,
But *B*[*aynar*]*d* never thought in all his Time:
Absolve him then from Guilt, his Soul is clean,
For he that never *thinks*, can nothing *mean*.

---

it is another manifestation of the fashionable dislike of the Society as seen in
such works as Butler's *Elephant in the Moon* and Shadwell's *Virtuoso*.

  * *See a late Pamphlet call'd*, The Transactioneer. (Original note.) A reference to one of the strange case histories which are scattered throughout the
Philosophical Transactions. The Matthews family ate something that turned
out to be dog-mercury. The next morning the man thought his chin was on fire
and "was forced to keep his hat full of water by him all the day long, and
frequently to dip his chin in it." One child slept from Thursday to Monday,
then died; the others were very sick, but we are not told their final fate. Sloane
quotes several authorities to show that the poison was undoubtedly dog-mercury:
"Mr. Ray in his history of plants calls it mercurialis perennis repens cynocrambe dicta, p. 163," etc. (*Philosophical Transactions*, abridged, edited by C.
Hutton, G. Shaw, R. Pearson, 1809, III [1683-94], 575-576.)

DV 30 (p. 16)

On the same, to a Friend who said Dr. B[aynar]d
Talk'd like an Apothecary.

Will, thou do'st much mistake the Doctor's Parts,
And wrong'st his Knowledge, and his great Deserts.
He mimicks no Discourse, or Talks by Rule,
But prattles like Himself, and that's a F[oo]l.

DV 31 (p. 16)

On the same Eternal Tatler.

B[aynar]d with noisie Cures may make us smile,
Yet cannot shew one Bill on any File:
What can it be that thus obstructs his Fame?
Because his Patients cannot say the same.
He on his own Report prescribes his Pills,
But Fame gives out, He neither Cures nor Kills.

* * *

CV 26 (p. 16)

To the Canting Author of the Satyr against Wit.

[—— Mildmay or Thomas Cheek?]

The Preacher *Maurus*[48] cries, all Wit is vain,
Unless 'tis like his Godliness, for Gain.
Of most vain Things he may the Folly own:
But Wit's a Vanity he has not known.

DV 32 (p. 16)

To a midnight Author who does not Cant I'll be Sworn.
That *C[heek?]*[49] Drinks hard, and late in Taverns sits,
'Tis known for *Truth* amongst the *B[o]w-street Wits*;
But I deny that Witness can be brought
That *C[heek?]* was ever Drunk with to much *Thought.*

* * *

[48] Blackmore.   [49] For Cheek's part in the quarrel see below, pp. 136-137.

CV 27 (pp. 16-17)

Friendly Advice to Dr. B[lackmore].

[Sir Henry Sheeres?]

Knighthood to Hero's only once was due,
Now's the Reward of Stupid Praise in you.
Why shou'd a Quack be dubb'd, unless it be
That pois'ning is an Act of Chivalry?
Thus we must own you have your Thousands slain
With the dire Stroks of your resistless Pen.
By whipping Boys your Cruelty began,
And grew by bolder Steps to killing Man.
Just the Reverse of *Dionysius* Fate,
Who fell to flogging Bums from murdering the State.
For both these Trades your Genius far unfit,
At length with sawcy Pride aspires to Wit.
Which by pretending to, you more Disgrace,
Than toasting *Beaus* our ancient *British* Race.
I'th Mountebank the Ass had lain conceal'd,
But his loud Braying has the Brute reveal'd.
Such vile Heroics, such unhallow'd Strains
Were never spawn'd before from *Irish* Brains.
Nor drowsy *Mum*, nor dozing *Usquebaugh*[50]
Cou'd e're suggest such Linesto Sir *John Daw.*[51]
You weakly Skirmish with the Sins o' th' Age,
And are the errant Scavinger o' th' Stage.
Why Virtue makes no Progress, now is plain,
Because such Knights as you its Cause maintain.
If you'd a Friend to Sense and Virtue be,
And to Mankind, for once be rul'd by me,
Leave Moralizing, Drugs and Poetry.

---

[50] *Mum,* a beer brewed at Brunswick and imported into England during the seventeenth and eighteenth centuries (*NED*, VI, 761). *Usquebaugh,* whiskey.
[51] A fool.

DV 33 (p. 16)

The Adviser *taken to Task.*

If Knighthood only be the *Hero's* Right,
What made a certain Man at *Will's*, a Knight,
Who never burn'd a Town, or gain'd a Fight?
Sir, you remember certainly what scores
Your Bombs defeated, of dull Sunburn'd *Moors*.
And how 'twas counted Valour to retreat,
And Nobler to be beaten than be beat.
Then pray deal fairly, and with Fame agree,
Owning the Justice of the Doctor's Plea;
Since *He* for saving many lives, is known,
When *Thou* just sav'dst thy self, and that is One.

DV 34 (p. 17)

To the same.

The Parliament who cry'd down Squibbs and Rockets,
Provided for our Safeties and our Pockets.
Not thinking Engineers in warlike times,
Instead of making Squibbs wou'd fall a making Rhimes.
But 'tis no matter, Knight, pursue thy Punns;
They'l do as little Mischief as thy Guns.

* * *

CV 28 (p. 17)

To Elkanah Settle,[52] *the City-Poet.*

[Tom Brown]

Wilt thou then passive see the Sacred Bays
Torn from thy Brows in thy declining Days,
And tamely let a Quack usurp thy Place,
So near *Guild-hall*, and in my Lord *May'r's* Face?
Rouze up for Shame, assert thy ancient Right,

---

[52] Taubman's successor, Elkanah Settle, was by some considered Dryden's rival.

And from his City-quarters drive the Knight.
Let Father* *Jordan* Martial Heat inspire,
And Unkle* *Tubman* fill thy Breast with Fire.
If *Bl*[*ackmo*]*re* cries, Both *Arthurs* are my own;
Quote thou the fam'd *Cambyses*, and Pope *Joan*.[53]
Cheapside at once two Bards can ne're allow,
But either He must Abdicate, or Thou.
Then if the Knight still keeps up his Pretence,
E'en turn Physician in thy own Defence.
'Tis own'd by all the Criticks of our Time,
Thou canst as well Prescribe, as *Bl*[*ackmo*]*re* Rhime.

DV 35 (p. 17)

To a Great Man who makes himself Little.

Were I to turn Physician, and prescribe
To certain P—— a most facetious Tribe,
I'de not make use of Syringes, and Tricks
To cure their Ulcers, and to mend their [——]
That Ladies *foul* might hug 'em intheir Arms,
And praise their Money, while They praise their Charms.

No, I'd another sort of Cure begin,
And leave their Running-Nags to smart for Sin,
As I prescrib'd *Restringents* in my Bills,
To cure the *running* Humours of their Quills,
And make 'em some more noble Frollick seek;
Not try to *write* that Sence, They cannot *speak*.

* * *

* *Two Famous City-Poets* (Original note.) The position of City Poet called for the writing of pageants for the Lord Mayor's shows, as well as panegyrics on the Lord Mayor elect. Needless to say, the Wits ridiculed this "laureateship" as they did almost everything connected with the City. Thomas Jordan, elected in 1671, was followed by Matthew Taubman.

[53] Settle's first play, *Cambyses* (1666), the first of a series of dramatic bombasts, was written at 18. In 1680 he published *The Female Prelate, being the History of the Life and Death of Pope Joan*. Long the butt of jokes, Settle received an undesirable immortality in the *Dunciad*.

CV 29 (p. 18)

To the Author of the Satyr against Wit, *upon
concealing his Name.*[54]

[Tom Brown]

He that in *Arthur's* Trash has Pennance done,
Needs not be told who writ this vile Lampoon.
In both the same eternal Dullness shines,
Inspires the Thoughts, and animates the Lines.
In both the same lewd Flattery we find,
The Praise defaming, and the Satyr kind.
Alike the Numbers, Fashion, and Design,
No Checquer-Tallies cou'd more nicely joyn.
Thy foolish Muse puts on her Mask too late,
We know the Strumpet by her Voice and Gate.

DV 36 (p. 18)

To T. B[rown] *upon His concealing his Name,
when He made the Author of the* Satyr against
Wit, *the Subject of his harmless Satyr for concealing His.*

Some Folks may write, and writing be conceal'd,
When such as *Thou* take pains to be reveal'd.
Scandal's a sort of Wit thou giv'st the Town,
And a *B*[*row*]*n*'s Works speak nothing but a *B*[*row*]*n*.
As thy lewd Muse with Infamy her Task
Cannot, because she's poor, provide a Mask.

No more than when her Master in a heat,
Resolving to be Cudgell'd, or to Beat;
For want of Cane-Man's Faith, and want of Pence,
Could get a Stick to shew his want of Sence.

*   *   *

[54] The poem was printed anonymously.

CV 30 (pp. 18-19)

On Job *newly Travestied by Sir* R[ichard] Bl[ackmore].

[Tom Brown]

Near *Lethe*'s Banks, where the forgetful Stream
With lazy Motion creeps, and seems to Dream,
Job with his thoughtful Friends discoursing sate
Of all the dark mysterious Turns of Fate:
And much they argued why Heaven's partial Care
The Good shou'd punish, and the Bad shou'd spare:
When lo! a Shade, new landed, forward prest,
And thus himself to listning *Job* Addrest:

Illustrious Ghost ! (I come not to upbraid)
Oh summon all thy Patience to thy Aid:
A *Cheapside* Quack, whose vile unhallow'd Pen
With equal Licence Murders Rhimes and Men,
In fumbling Fustian has burlesqu'd thy Page,
And fam'd *Jack D[u]nt[o]n* [55] brings it on the Stage,
Was ever Man, the patient *Job* did cry,
So plagu'd with cursed Messengers, as I?
All other Losses, unconcern'd I bore,
But never heard such Stabbing News before.
Who can behold the Issue of his Brain
Mangled by barbarous Hands, and not complain?
This scribbling Quack (his Fame I know too well
By Thousand Ghosts whom he has sent to Hell)
Dull *Satan*'s feebler Malice will refine,
And Stab me through and through in every Line.
The Devil more brave, did open War declare,
The fawning Poet kills, and speaks me fair.
Curs'd be the Wretch, that taught him first to Write,
And with lewd Pen and Ink indulg'd his Spite:
That fly-blow'd the young Bard with buzzing Rhymes,

[55] A bookseller.

And fill'd his tender Ears with *Grubstreet* Chimes.
Curs'd be the Paper-Mill his Muse employs,
Curs'd be the Sot who on his Skill relies.

Thus *Job* complain'd, but to forget his Grief,
In *Lethe*'s Sov'raign Streams he sought Relief.

DV 37 (p. 18)

To the same [Tom Brown].

Job, as thou say'st, being willing to forget
The Cause, for which thou mad'st him storm and fret,
Plung'd into *Lethe*'s Streams to seek relief,
And lost the sad remembrance of his Grief.

But take my word, Sir *Richard* need not use
That method for the Scandal of thy Muse:
For what e're flows from such a triffling Sot,
Dies of it *self*, and's born to be *forgot*.

DV 38 (p. 19)

To the same [Tom Brown].

Tom, take my word, thou'st done like Man of Skill,
And I applaud the Conquest of thy Quill;
The *Wife* and *Satan* fail'd in *Their* design;
But thou had'st brought their *Wish* about in thine.
Thou teachest *Job* most *heartily* to *Curse*;
Satan cou'd ne're have taught him what was worse.

So well thou'st play'd the subtle Tempter's part;
Yet he must give precedence to thy Art.
As full of Wonder we can neither grant,
Or *Job* the greater *Fiend*, or *B*[*row*]*n* the greater *Saint*.

*   *   *

CV 31 (p. 19)

To Sir R[ichard] Bl[ackmore] *upon his Unhappy Talent
at Praising and Railing.*

[Tom Brown or Dr. Smalwood?]

Thine is the only Muse in *British* Ground
Whose Satyr tickles, and whose Praises wound:
Sure *Hebrew* first was taught her by her Nurse,
Where the same Word is used to Bless and Curse.

DV 39 (p. 19)

To an Epigrammatic Parson.

'Tis false, leud Priest, I speak it to thy Face,
As are thy Actions infamous and base.
His Satyr tickle?   No, it cannot be;
Especially that part which touches Thee.

Wounds almost cur'd, Experience will teach,
May have a Titillation, and an Itch.
But as for *Thine,* I'de have *Thee* rest assur'd,
Thou'l ne're be *tickled,* who can'st ne're be *cur'd.*

*   *   *

CV 32 (pp. 20-21)

To Dr. Garth, *on the Fourth Edition of his
incomparable Poem,* The Dispensary; *Occasion'd
by some Lines in the* Satyr against Wit.

[Dr. James Drake]

Bold thy Attempt, in these hard Times to raise
In our unfriendly Clime the tender Bays,
While Northern Blasts drive from the Neighb'ring Flood,
And nip the springing Lawrel in the Bud.
On such bleak Paths our present Poets tread,
The very Garland withers on each Head.

In vain the Critics strive to Purge the Soil,
Fertile in Weeds it mocks their busie Toil.
Spontaneous Crops of *Jobs* and *Arthurs* rise,
Whose tow'ring Non-sense braves the very Skies:
Like Paper-kites the empty Volumes fly,
And by meer force of Wind are rais'd on high.

While we did these with stupid Patience spare,
And from *Apollo's* Plants withdrew our Care,
The *Muses* Garden did small Product yield,
But Hemp, and Hemlock over-ran the Field;
'Till skilful *Garth*, with Salutary Hand,
Taught us to Weed, and Cure Poetic Land,
Grubb'd up the Brakes, and Thistles, which he found,
And sow'd with Verse, and Wit the Sacred Ground.
But Now the Riches of that Soil appear,
Which Four fair Harvests yields in Half a Year.

No more let Critics of the Want complain
Of *Mantuan* Verse, or the *Mæonian* Strain;
Above them *Garth* do's on their Shoulders rise,
And, what our Language wants, his Wit supplies.
Fam'd Poets after him shall strain their Throats,
And unfledg'd Muses chirp their Infant-notes.

Yes *Garth*: thy Enemies confess thy Store,
They burst with Envy, yet they long for more:
Ev'n we, thy Friends, in doubt thy Kindness call,
To see thy Stock so large, and Gift so small.
But Jewels in small Cabinets are laid,
And richest Wines in little Casks convey'd.

Let lumpish *Bl*[*ackmo*]*re* his dull Hackney freight,
And break his Back with heavy Folio's weight.
His *Pegasus* is of the *Flanders* Breed,
And Limb'd for Draught, or Burthen, not for Speed.

With Cart-horse Trot he sweats beneath the Pack
Of Rhiming Prose, and Knighthood on his Back:
Made for a Drudge, e'en let him beat the Road,
And tug of sensless Rheams th' Heroic Load;
Till overstrain'd the Jade is set, and tires,
And sinking in the Mud with Groans expires.

Then *Bl[ackmo]re* shall this Favour owe to thee,
That thou perpetuat'st his Memory.
Bavius and *Maevius* so their Works survive,
And in one single Line of *Virgil's* live.

DV 40 (pp. 20-21)

A Consolatory Paper of Verses to Dr. D[ra]ke,
   upon the News that He Commended the 4th. *Edition
   of Dr.* Garth's *Dispensary, and could not get His
   own Translation of* Herodotus *to bear* One.[56]

Bold thy attempt, let Truth and Friendship speak,
In these *dull* Times to venture forth at *Greek*.
And dare *Construe* and *Translate* with speed,
What Gentlemen of *Practice* cou'd not *read*.

Yet as Success not always waits the Brave,
And Heroes lose the Laurel for the Grave;
So tho' thy Volumes by their Bulk Disclose,
What havock thou ha'st made of Sense and Prose.
Yet to our sorrow We, thy Friends, behold
Thy Price beat down, and ev'ry Sheet unfold;
While other Versions are receiv'd and bought,
Pigmies in *Mischief* to the *Giant* thought.

However, Man, take heart of Oak, and dare
Ev'n still to shew the World thy *stupid* Care,

---

[56] Apparently Drake's *Herodotus* was never published. However, it might be pointed out that Blackmore too had a hand in an unsuccessful translation of Herodotus (see above, p. 51, n. 12).

To mangle other's Works thy time employ,
Fools may, perhaps, at last be found to buy;
And thou acknowledg'd with thy skilful Pen,
As fit to murther *Sense*, as murther *Men*.

O *D*[*ra*]*ke*! How great shall be thy future Name?
What multitudes of *Trunks* shall speak thy Fame!
Band-Box shall in thy Vindication rise,
And many a Cook with thee defend his Pies,
Which otherwise (I'm to thy merit just)
Would never tempt *Young Children* with their *Crust*.

Then take Thy Pen, as Men of Letters shou'd,
And Scrible for succeeding Trader's good.
What! If some certain Booksellers agree
Not to be Broke by such a Scribe as Thee,
'Tis Ten to One, but Thou a Chap may'st find
Among the Trading sort of Human Kind,
Who for the sake of dealing once in Greek,
Will take it off Thy hands, and nobly *break*.

Arise then, Friend, and reassume thy Pen,
And swear B— G-d, 'tis good, like Antient *Ben*;
Like a true Author magnifie thy Pains,
And tell *Ben T*[*oo*]*k*[*e*] [57] he has no Guts in's Brains,
Who durst such *useful Knowledge* to decry,
He cannot *understand* who does not *buy*.

These are the ways preceding Writers us'd
When once flung by, and Their *own* Price refus'd,
And These, my Friend, are what the *present* tread,
As soon as slighted and return'd unread.

---

[57] Benjamin Tooke, a bookseller in London from 1669 to 1716, was one of the largest publishers of the day and Swift's bookseller (Henry R. Plomer, *Dictionary of the Printers and Booksellers Who Were at Work in England, Scotland, and Ireland from 1668 to 1725*, Bibliographical Society, Oxford, 1922, p. 293).

Curse ev'ry thing in Print which has Success,
Make Author's write, and Readers buy, by guess;
Like Paper Kites, let *other's Labour's fly,*
And by mere force of Wind be *born on high.*
But rest assur'd, and easie in Thy Mind,
Thy Volumes dare the most Tempestuous Wind,
Though *North* and *South,* and each contending Blast
Should in united Storms their Furies cast,
Unmov'd by Force, and uninform'd by Sence,
Stupidity shall be their safe Defence;
Fix'd to their Shelv's no Winds can make 'em rise,
And their Thou'lt let 'em lie if thou art wise.

* * *

CV 33 (pp. 21-22)

On Sir R[ichard] Bl[ackmo]re's *Noble Project to Erect*
a Bank of Wit.[58]

[Tom Brown]

The Thought was great, and worthy of a Cit,[59]
In present Dearth, to erect a Bank of Wit.
Thus breaking Trades-men, ready for a Jayl,
Raise Millions for our Senate o're their Ale.
But thou'rt declar'd a Bankrupt, and thy Note
Even in old *Grub-street* scarce wou'd fetch a Groat.
Apollo scorns thy Project, and the *Nine* [60]
With Indignation laugh at thy Design.
There's not a Trader to the Sacred *Hill*
But knows thy Wants, and would Protest thy Bill;

---

[58] Let us erect a Bank for Wit and Sense.
A Bank whose current Bills may Payment make,
Till new Mill'd Wit shall from the Mint come back.
(*Satyr against Wit,* p. 10.)
[59] Citizen. The Wits liked to poke fun at those who lived in the city;
Blackmore was called the City Bard.
[60] The Nine Muses.

Thy Credit can't a Farthing there Command,
Though *Fr[e]ke* and *R[y]m[e]r* [61] shou'd thy Sureties
stand.

*   *   *

DV 41 (p. 22)

To Mr. F[rancis] M[anning] *on his Incomprehensible*
Farce, *which goes by the Name of the* Generous
Choice.

By a Lady.

Thy Thoughts were never *great*, it's very plain,
By this poor Trifling product of Thy Brain;
But I, in question do my Judgment call,
If Thou had'st Brains, Thou would'st not write at all.

DV 42 (p. 22)

To the same, on his Poem, call'd Greenwich-Hill.
By another Lady.

Lawyer, and Bard, believe me for Thy Friend,
If I Thy stupid Poem don't Commend.
The Lady's are Indebted to Thy Quill,
And *Greenwich* must acknowledge Thy good will;
But now Thou'st prais'd 'em both, dear Scribbler see,
If any Fool will do the *same* by *Thee.*

*   *   *

---

[61] William Freke, who thought of himself as a mystic, was jeered at by the
Wits for his dream dictionary and religious writings. He finally went insane;
Thomas Rymer took an extreme stand on the unities. His absurd remarks about
Shakespeare's plays (particularly *Othello*) still make him a laughingstock of
critics.

CV 34 (pp. 22-23)

To Sir R[ichard] Bl[ackmo]re, *on the two Wooden Horses before* Sadlers-hal.[62]

[Tom Brown]

As trusty Broom-staff Midnight Witch bestrides,
When on some Grand Dispatch of Hell she rides,
O're gilded Pinacles, and lofty Towers,
And tallest Pines with furious hast she scowrs.
Out flies in her Career the lab'ring Wind,
And sees spent Exhalations lag behind.
Arriving at the Black *Divan* at last
In some drear Wood, or solitary Wast:
The Fiend her cheated Senses does delude,
With airy Visions of imagin'd Food.
Ev'n so, dear Knight, (my Freedom you'll Excuse,
If to a Witch I have compar'd your Muse)
Ev'n so on Wooden Prancer, mounted high,
Your Muse takes nimble Journeys in the Sky.
When in her boldest Strains, and highest Flights,
She Sings of strange Adventures, and Exploits,
Battles, Enchantments, Furies, Devils, and Knights;
When she at *Arthur*'s Fairy Table dines,
And high-pil'd Dishes sees, and generous Wines.

'Twas kindly done of the good-natur'd Cits
To Place before thy Door a Brace of Tits.[63]
For *Pegasus* wou'd ne're endure the weight
Of such a Quibbling, Scribbling, Dribbling Knight:

---

[62] There are numerous references in *Commendatory Verses* to these wooden horses. One writer has suggested an explanation: " Two horses, *argent*, . . . are the supporters of the Company's arms " (H. B. Wheatley, *London Past and Present*, 1891, III, 198). The evidence given in this poem and others would seem to point to the fact that there actually were two such horses in front of the hall.

[63] *Tit*, a small horse, used in a derogatory sense, a nag (*NED*, X, pt. 1, 72).

That generous Steed, rather than gaul his Back
With a Pedantic Bard, and Nauseous Quack,
Wou'd kneel to take a Pedlar and his Pack,

DV 43 (p. 23)

A Pun, by Mr. D—— P——
To T[OM] B[ROWN] *upon his Witches* Trusty *Broomstaff.*

By all the Punns that D——l ever made,
Most wisely fitted, and most bravely said,
Broomstaff must own, if Broomstaff had a Tongue,
It owes it's chiefest glory to thy Song.
Trusty's a Noble Epithet, and Safe,
A Witch can never fall from such a Staff:
But Thou must own, if Thoud'st to Truth be just,
Thoud'st sooner giv't a *Vintner*, if He'd *Trust.*

DV 44 (p. 23)

To the same, by one who is Free of the
Sadler's *Company.*

That we have wooden Horses at our Doors,
Is full as True as Thine has Chalks and Scores,
Our's stand without, but *Thomas*, 'tis no Sin,
To say, Thy Garrat has an A——ss within.

* * *

CV 35 (p. 23)

To a Famous Doctor and Poet at Sadlers-hall.

If Wit (as we are told) be a Disease,
And if Physicians Cure by Contraries:
Bl[ackmo]re alone the healing Secret knows,
'Tis from his Pen the grand *Elixir* flows.

DV 45 (p. 23)

To the Infamous Poetaster at Will's *Coffee-House.*

If Wit (as Thou art told) is a Disease,
Thou need'st not give Sir *R*[*ichard*] *Bl*[*ackmo*]*re* Fees,
For ev'ry Fool, with any Brains, must own,
He cannot Purge off Humours, where are none.

* * *

CV 36 (pp. 23-24)

To· the Cheapside *Quack: occasion'd by this Verse
in the* Satyr against Wit,

"Who with more ease can cure than *C*[*olbat*]*ch* kill"

By a Gentleman whom Dr. C[o]lb[at]ch [64] *had cur'd
of the Gout.*

[Col. Johnson]

How durst thy railing Muse, vain Wretch, pretend
In base Lampoon thus to abuse my Friend!
Whose Sacred Art has freed me from my Pains,
And broke a haughty Tyrant's stubborn Chains?
Keep off, for if thou com'st within my Clutches,
I'll bast thy Knighthood with my Quondam Crutches.
The generous Wine that does my Sorrows drown,
The charming *Cælia* that my Nights does crown,
The manly Pleasures of the sporting Fields,
The gay Delights the pompous *Drama* yields,
All this, and more to his great Skill I owe,
Such Blessings can thy Boasted Helps bestow?
The Snuff of Life perhaps thy feeble Art
May fondly lengthen to thy Patient's smart.
But Health no more 'tis in thy Power to give,
Than thy dull Muse can make her Heroes live.

---

[64] Sir John Colbatch was one of the signers of the Dispensary project.

Ev'n War and Plague of Killing, to arraign
In thee, is most nonsensical and vain.
Thee, who a branded Killer art declar'd,
In both Capacities of Quack and Bard.
Whatever Sots to thy Prescriptions fly,
For their vain Confidence are sure to die:
And whate'er Argument thy Muse employs,
Her awkward stupid Management destroys.
Death with sure steps thy Doses still attends,
And Death too follows whom thy *Muse* commends.
What can escape thy All-destroying Quill,
When ev'n thy Cordials, and thy Praises kill?
Thy Mother sure, when in Despair and Pain
She brought thee forth, thought of the Murd'rer *Cain*.

DV 46 (p. 24)

To the Gentleman whom Dr. C[o]lb[at]ch
   Cur'd of the Gout.

Sir, If you'd shew the Doctor's Worth and Skill,
Ask Him, who Cur'd your *Legs* to cure your *Quill*,
And You will never Write so cursed Ill.

DV 47 (p. 24)

To the same.

Sir, We Rejoice to hear that You are sound,
That you drink Wine, and send the Glasses round;
That Punks no more your want of Strength upbraid,
But all Love's reck'nings now are fully paid.
E'en take the Manly Pleasures of the Field,
And follow the Delights which *Drama*'s yield.
But be Advis'd, and once, I beg You, think,
Quit the Debauches of Leud Pen and Ink.
The Doctor's Mother Thought, 'tis very plain
Amongst Her Childbed Pangs, and felt the Pain;

But Your's ne're Thought at all, I durst believe,
By the few signs of *Thought* Your Writings give.

* * *

CV 37 (p. 24)

*To that most incomparable Bard and Quack, the
   Author of the* Satyr against Wit.

[Thomas Creech or Thomas Cheek?]

I Charge thee, Knight, in great Apollo's Name, ⎫
If thou'rt not dead to all Reproof and Shame,   ⎬
Either thy Rhimes, or Clysters to disclaim.   ⎭
Both are too much one feeble Brain to rack,
Besides the Bard will soon undo the Quack.
Such Shoals of Readers thy damn'd Fustian kills,
Thou'lt scarce leave one alive to take thy Pills.

DV 48 (p. 24)

*To the Blustring Poet, who never Spoke or Wrote
   any thing that was taken notice of before.*

I Tell Thee Man, thy Charges I defie,
Stradle and Damn Thy self, why, what care I.
Put off the Fool, and he'll put off his Rhimes,
For *Fool*'s make *Poets* in our Senceless Times:
Be *Wise* in Day-time, and be *Chast* at Night,
And That's the way to make Him *cease* to *Write*.

* * *

CV 38 (p. 25)

Epigram upon King ARTHUR.

[Tom Brown]

The *British Arthur*, as Historians tell,
Deriv'd his Birth from *Merlin's* Magic Spell.
When *Uter*, taking the wrong'd Husband's Shape,
On fair *Igerne* did commit a Rape.

But modern *Arthur* of the *Cheapside* Line,
May justly boast his Parentage Divine.
Wearing thy Phyz, and in thy Habit drest,
The God of Dullness his lewd Dam comprest.

DV 49 (p. 25)

An Epigram on T[o]m B[row]n.

How *B[row]n* was *born* in *Garret* or in *Cell*,
Let those determine who can better tell;
Or for what Ends the vengeful Heav'ns design'd
This *Pestilence* of Wit and human Kind:
But this I dare affirm, without a Lie,
His *Epigrams* are only *born* to *die*.

DV 50 (p. 25)

On the same.

If *Arthur* from a *Ravish'd* Parent came,
Thy *Ballad's* merry *Birth* is much the same;
For Thou (believe it Bard without Offence)
Writing, dost still commit a *Rape* on *Sense*.

* * *

CV 39 (p. 25)

A merry Ballad on the City Bard,

To a New Play-house Tune.

[Richard Norton]

In *London* City near *Cheapside*
    A wondrous Bard does dwell,
Whose *Epics* (if they're not bely'd)
    Do *Virgil's* far excell:
A sprightly Wit, and Person joyn'd,
    Both Poet and Physician:
Artist as famous in his kind,

For ought I know, as *Titian*.
In Coffee-houses purest Air
  His foggy Lines he Writes:
In Fields of Dust and Spittle there
  His *British* Hero Fights.
By sudden Motion then o'reta'ne,
  The Privy-house he chooses:
Great are his Thoughts, and great his Pain,
  And yet no Time he loses.
Grip'd in his Guts and Muse, he there Indites,
And Praises *Arthur* most, when most he Sh——.

DV 51 (p. 25)

An Epigram flung away on a certain
Ballad-making Senator.

Where *N*[*orto*]*n* lives I cannot tell,
  If ne'er so fain I wou'd;
But *N*[*orto*]*n* this *I know full well*,
Wher'er the *Maggot* makes you dwell,
  You'll never do *much good*.

* * *

CV 40 (pp. 26-28)

An Epitome of a Poem, truly call'd, A Satyr against Wit;
done for the Undeceiving of some Readers, who have
mistaken the Panegyrick in that Immortal Work for the
Satyr, and the Satyr for the Panegyrick.

[Tom Brown]

Who can forbear and tamely silent sit,	*l*. 1. *p.* 3
And see his Native Land *as void* of Wit [65]	*l*. 2
As every Piece the City-Knight has Writ?	
How happy were the old unpolish'd Times,	*l*. 13

---

[65] Undone by Wit (*Satyr against Wit*). In the *Epitome* the italicized portions are those changed or added by Tom Brown. The page and line references are also his.

As free from Wit, as other Modern Crimes, *l.* 14
And what is more from, Bl[ackmo]re's *nauseous Rhimes.*
As our Fore-Fathers Vig'rous were and Brave, *l.* 15
So they were Virtuous, Wise, Discreet and Grave, *l.* 16
And wou'd have call'd our Quack a fawning Slave.[66]
Clodpate, by *Banks,* and *Stocks,* and *Projects* bit, *l.* 5. *p.* 5
Turns up his Whites, and *in his Pious Fit,* *l.* 6
He *Cheats* and *Prays,* a certain sign of *Cit.*[67] *l.* 7
Craper runs madly 'midst the thickest Crowd, *l.* 8
Sometimes says nothing, sometimes talks aloud.[68]
Under the Means he lies, frequents the Stage, *l.* 10
Is very lewd, and does at Learning rage; *l.* 11
And this vile Stuff we find in every Page.
A Bant'ring Spirit, has our Men posse.st, *l.* 20
And Wisdom is become a standing Jest, *l.* 21
Which is a burning Shame I do protest.
Wit does of Virtue sure Destruction make, *l.* 22
Who can produce a Wit, and not a Rake? *l.* 23
A Challenge started ne're but by a Quack.
The Mob of Wits is up to storm the Town, *l.* 1. *p.* 6
To pull all Virtue and right Reason down, *l.* 2
Then to surprize the Tower, and steal the Crown,[69]
And the lewd Crew affirm, by all that's good, *l.* 15
They'll ne're disperse till they have *B[lackmo]re's*[70]
  Blood; *l.* 16
But they'll ne're have his Brains, by good King Lud.
For that *industrious Bard of Late*[71] has done *l.* 16. *p.* 6

---

[66] Detecting both alike the Wit and Knave (*Satyr against Wit*).

[67] By Pox and Hunger and by *D[ryde]n* bit
  He grins and snarles, and in his dogged Fit
  Froths at the Mouth, a certain Sign of Wit.
          (*Satyr against Wit*)

[68] And fain wou'd be infected, if he cou'd (*Satyr against Wit*).

[69] Quite to subvert Religion's sacred Fence,
  To set up Wit, and pull down Common Sense.
          (*Satyr against Wit*)

[70] *B[ent]l[e]y's* (*Satyr against Wit*).

[71] For that ill-natur'd Critic has undone (*Satyr against Wit*).

The rarest Piece of Wit that e're was shown,   *l.* 17
And publish'd Dogg'rel he's asham'd to own.[72]
The Skilful *T*[*y*]*s*[*o*]*n*'s [73] Name they dare Invade,   *l.* 31. *p.* 6
And yet they are undone without his Aid;   *l.* 2
Did they read thee, I shou'd conclude them Mad.
T[*y*]*s*[*o*]*n* with base Reproaches they pursue,   *l.* 1. *p.* 7
Just as his *Moor-fields* Patients us'd to do,   *l.* 4
Who give to T[y]s[o]n, *what is* T[y]s[o]n'*s due.*
Wit does enfeeble and debauch the Mind,   *l.* 7
Before to Business or to Arts inclin'd: *l.* 8
Then thou wilt never be Debauch'd, I find.
Had *S*[*ome*]*rs*, *H*[*ol*]*t*, or *T*[*reb*]*y*, who with awe
                                                  l. 15, 16, 17, 18
We Name, been Wits, they Ne're had learn'd the Law.[74]
But sure this Compliment's not worth a Straw.
The Law will ne're support the bant'ring Breed,   *l.* 22
Tho' *Blockheads* may, yet Wits can ne're succeed,[75]   *l.* 23
For which Friend Sl[oa]ne *I hope will break thy Head.*
R[*atcli*]*ff*[*e*] has wit and lavishes away   *l.* 24

---

[72] The *Satyr against Wit* was published anonymously.

[73] Dr. Edward Tyson, physician to Bridewell and Bethlehem hospitals, was a prolific writer on medical and natural history subjects. Because he was on the side of the apothecaries in the Dispensary quarrel, Garth pilloried him in the *Dispensary* under the name of Carus:

> His Spirits stagnate like *Cocitus's* Flood,
> And nought but Calentures can warm his Blood
> In his chill Veins the sluggish Puddle flows,
> And loads with lazy Fogs his sable Brows.
> Legions of Lunaticks about him press,
> 'Tis he that can lost Intellects redress . . .
> But each vile Scribler's happy on this score,
> He'll find some *Carus* still to read him o're (IV, p. 30).

[74] Can Wit supply great T[re]by's nervous Sense?
> Or S[ome]r's more than Roman Eloquence?
> Which way has H[ol]t gain'd Universal Fame?
>   (*Satyr against Wit*)

Sir John Holt (1642-1710) and Sir George Treby (1644?-1700) were well-known judges.

[75] A Sl[oane] may sometimes there, but Wits can ne'er succeed (*Satyr against Wit*).

So much in nauseous Northern Brogue each day,
As wou'd suffice to Damn a Smithfield-*Play.*[76]
Wit does our Schools and Colleges invade,　　　*l.* 20. *p.* 8
And has of Letters vast Destruction made,　　　　*l.* 21
But that it spoils thy Learning, can't be said.
That such a Failure no Man may incense,　　　*l.* 17. *p.* 10
Let us erect a Bank for Wit and Sense:　　　　*l.* 18
And so set up at other Mens Expence.
Let S[ome]r[s] D[orse]t, S[heffie]ld, M[onta]gue　*l.* 21
Lend but their Names the Project then will do:　*l.* 22
What! Lend *'em such a Bankrupt Wretch as you.*
Duncombs and *Claytons*[77] *of Parnassus* all,　　　*l.* 27
Who cannot sink, unless the Hill shou'd fall,　　*l.* 28
Why then, they need but go to Sadlers-hall.[78]
St. E[vre]m[on]t, to make the thing compleat,　*l.* 21. *p.* 9
No English *knows, and therefore* is most fit[79]
To oversee the Coining of our Wit.　　　　　　*l.* 22
Nor shall M——rs, W——tt, Ch[a]rl[e]tt be forgot,[80]
With solid *Fr[e]ke*[81] and *R[yme]r and who Not?*
Then all our Friends the Actions shall cry up,　*l.* 6. *p.* 12
And all the railing Mouths of Envy stop.　　　　*l.* 7

---

[76] More in his Conversion every Day
Than wou'd supply a modern Writer's Play
(*Satyr against Wit*)

[77] Sir Charles Duncombe and Sir Robert Clayton were known for their great wealth. Each became Lord Mayor and Clayton was director of the Bank of England.

[78] Where Blackmore lived.

[79] St. E[vre]m[ont] and R[yme]r both are fit (*Satyr against Wit*).

[80] It has been suggested that this may be Dr. Arthur Charlett. King's chaplain and master of University College, Oxford, Charlett died in 1722. Charlett was Codrington's friend and the one who notified Codrington of his friend Creech's death (Harlow, *Christopher Codrington*, pp. 62-63). He also approved of the Dispensary (for a letter from Garth to Charlett see *Letters Written by Eminent Persons in the Seventeenth and Eighteenth Centuries* (London, 1813), I, 114. It does not seem likely that a person so close to Codrington and his circle would be linked, as he is in this passage, with Freke and Rymer.

[81] A religious mystic who went insane. See above, p. 112, n. 61.

Wou'd we cou'd Padlock thine, Eternal Fop.
The Project then will *T*[*albo*]*tts* Test abide,   *l.* 11. *p.* 16
And with his Mark please all the World beside.   *l.* 12
But dare thy Arthurs by this Test be tried?
Then what will *D*[*ry*]*d*[*e*]*n*, *G*[*art*]*h*, or
    C[*o*]*ng*[*re*]*ve* say   *l.* 27. *p.* 9
When all their wicked Mixture's purg'd away?   *l.* 28
Thy Metal's baser than their worst Allay.
What will become of *S*[*ou*]*th*[*er*]*n*[*e*], *W*[*y*]*ch*[*erl*]*y*   *l.* 29
Who by this means will grievous Sufferers be? [82]   *l.* 30
No matter, they'l ne're send a Brief to Thee.
All these debauch'd by *D*[*ryde*]*n* and his Crew   *l.* 22. *p.* 12
Turn Bawds to Vice, and wicked Aims pursue: *l.* 23
To hear thee Cant wou'd make ev'n B[urge]ss [83]
    Spew.
For now an honest Man can't peep abroad,   *l.* 9. *p.* 13
Nor a chast Muse, *but whip They bring a Rod.*[84]   *l.* 16
E'n *Atticus* himself these Men wou'd Curse,   *l.* 5. *p.* 14
Shou'd *Atticus* appear without his Purse,   *l.* 6
If this be Praise, what Libel can say Worse?
Nay *Darfell* too, shou'd he forbear to treat,   *l.* 7. *p.* 14
These Men that cry him up, their Words wou'd
    Eat,[85]   *l.* 8
And say in Scorn, He had no Brains to beat.

[82] 'Tis true, that when the course and worthless Dross
    Is purg'd away, there will be mighty Loss.
    Ev'n *C*[*ongrev*]*e*, *S*[*outher*]*n*[*e*], *Manly W*[*ycher*]*ly*,
    When thus refin'd will grievous Suff'rers be.
                    (*Satyr against Wit*)
[83] Daniel Burgess, famous dissenting preacher.
[84] And all chast Muses dread the dangerous Road (*ibid.*).
[85] They cry up *Darfel* for a Wit, to treat
    Let him forbear, and they their Words will eat (*ibid.*).

DV 52 (pp. 25-28)

Notes on the two Celebrated Copies in the
 Commendatory Verses, to let the Reader know the
 difference between the faithfulness of
 their Epitome and our Copies; taken verbatim
 from their own Words, without the omission
 of one Line.

By Nature meant, by Want a Pedant made,
Bl[*ackmo*]*re* at first set up the Whipping-Trade,
   Had'st Thou been whipp'd Thou ne'er would'st Schools
   upbraid.
Grown fond of Buttocks he would lash no more,
But kindly cur'd the A——se he gall'd before:
   And prithee where's the Sin to cure a Sore?
So Quack commenc'd; thence fierce with Pride he swore
That Tooth-Ach, Gripes, and Corns, should be no more;
   Had he said Fops, thoud'st call his Mother Whore.
In vain his Drugs, as well as Birch he try'd,
His Boys grew Block-heads, and his Patients dy'd,
   Then Thou hast got the Block-heads on thy Side.
Next he turn'd Bard and mounted on a Cart,
Whose hideous Rumbling made *Apollo* start;
   Doubtless thy Coachman drives with Ease and Art.
Burlesqu'd the bravest, wisest Son of *Mars*,
In Ballad-Rhimes and all the Pomp of Farce,
   A Commendation fit to wipe his A——se.
Still he chang'd Callings, and at length has hit ⎫
On Business, for his matchless Talent fit   ⎬
To give us Drenches for the Plague of Wit.   ⎭
Thou need'st no Drench *take* Bl[ackmo]re's *Word for it.*
Bold thy Attempt in these hard Times to raise
In our unfriendly Clime the tender Bays,
   But bolder thine thy Country to dispraise.
While Northern Blasts drive from the neighb'ring Flood,

And nip the springing Lawrel in the Bud;
That thine e'er sprung I never understood.
On such bleak Paths our present Poets tread,
The very Garland withers on each Head,
When thou hast none to wither, as it's said.
In vain the Criticks strive to Purge the Soil,
Fertile in Weeds it mock's their busy Toil,
And D[ra]ke*'s shoot up to be a* C[olli]er*'s Foyl.*
Spontaneous Crops of *Job*'s and *Arthur*'s rise,
Whose tow'ring Nonsense braves the very Skies,
While poor Herodotus *unprinted lies.*
Like Paper-Kites the empty Volumes fly,
And by meer force of Wind are rais'd on high;
Thy Works would do the same if T[oo]ke *would buy.*
While we did these with stupid Patience spare,
And from *Apollo*'s Plants withdraw our Care;
The Plants far'd ne'er the worse I durst to swear.
The Muses Garden did small Product yield,
And Hemp and Hemlock over-ran the Field;
I warrant 'twas because thou laid'st conceal'd.
'Till skilful *Garth* with Salutary Hand,
Taught us to Weed and Cure Poetick Land;
But thou ne'er learnd'st the Cure I understand.
Grubb'd up the Brakes and Thistles which he found,
And sow'd with Verse and Wit the sacred Ground,
Not Verse and Wit like thine, which cannot wound.
But now the Riches of that Soil appear,
Which four fair Harvests yield in half a Year;
Four more than thy Translation e'er will bear.
No more let Criticks of the Want complain,
Of *Mantuan* Verse or the *Mæonian* Strain:
For those two Books are in the Press again.
Above 'em *Garth* does on their Shoulders rise,
And, what our Language wants, his Wit supplies;
Who says the same of Thine by Heaven lies.
Fam'd Poets after him shall stretch their Throats,

And unfledg'd Muses chirp their Infant Notes;
 Unfledg'd I guess because they have no Coats.
Yes *Garth*; thy Enemies confess thy Store,
They burst with *Envy*, yet they *long* for more,
 A sort of Envy never known before.
Ev'n we, thy Friends, in doubt thy Kindness call,
To see thy Stock so large and Gift so small;
 Some Folks had lik'd him, if no Gift at all.
But Jewels in small Cabinets are laid,
And richest Wines in little Casks convey'd;
 Thou seldom drink'st those Wines I am afraid.
Let lumpish *Bl[ackmo]re* his dull Hackney F[r]eight,
And *break* his *Back* with heavy Folio's Weight,
 For which if I were He, I'd break thy Pate.
His *Pegasus* is of the *Flanders* Breed,
And Limb'd for Draught or Burthen, not for Speed;
 A Sign his Strength of Thought does thine exceed.
With Cart-Horse Trot he sweats beneath the Pack
Of Rhiming Prose, and Knighthood on his Back;
 A Burthen thou'lt ne'er have, malicious Quack.
Made for a Drudge e'en let him beat the Road,
And tug of sensless Reams th'heroick Load;
 Thou hast Reams by thee cannot get abroad.
'Till overstrain'd, the Jade is set, and tires,
And sinking in the Mud with Groans expires:
 Who say thy Muse can sink are errant Lyars.
Then *Bl[ackmo]re* shall this Favour owe to Thee;
That thou perpetuatest his Memory;
 Collier *has done the very same for Thee.*
Bavius and *Mœvius* so their Works survive,
And in one single Line of *Virgil*'s live;
 A Gift which all Thy Lines can never give.

* * *

CV 41 (pp. 29-30)

A Lent-Entertainment: Or, A Merry Interview by Moon-light, betwixt a Ghost and the City-Bard.[86]

PHœbus the witty, gay and bright,
Was sunk beneath his tedious Light,
And *Nature* had her Curtain's drawn
O're half the World of Sable-lawn;
The *Fairies* in the gloomy Shade
Danc'd Minuets, while *Hobgoblins* play'd;
The weary *Clown* with Toil opprest
Renews his Strength by grateful Rest;
Not so the Bosoms of the *Great*,
Whom Guilt and Cares corrode and eat,
This swets beneath *Ambition*'s Itch,
And that by *Frauds* and *Rapines* rich;
'Tother profusely wastes his Time,
Nay *cracks* his Brains to get a *Rhime*;
While *various* Mortals thus contrive
By Blood, and Factions how to thrive;
No smaller Pangs our *Doctor* seiz'd
How to scan *Verse*, than cure *Diseas'd*;
He long implor'd *Apollo*'s Aid,
To save the *Sick*, and sing the *Dead*;
(To him both Attributes are due
Of *Poet*, and *Physician* too)
The angry *God* his Incense spurn'd,
And in a Fury from him turn'd.
While the neglected *Altars* smoakt.
The *Priest* himself was almost choakt:
The *Bard*, sunk down with his Despair,

---

[86] This poem is the only addition to the 30-page version of *Commendatory Verses*; it is printed in double columns on a single sheet and added to the original 28 pages. Since it is the only poem for which there is no reply in *Discommendatory Verses*, it is likely that the 30-page version of *Commendatory Verses* appeared after *Discommendatory Verses*. See above, p. 43.

Blasphem'd all Wit, and tore his Hair:
But yet his Folly to evince,
He with *King Arthur* backt his *Prince*,
And humbly begging both their Aids,
He thus addrest the Royal Shades:

Ye mighty *Heroes* of your Times,
Who cannot *Dye* but by my *Rhimes*;
'Tis too too much that you shou'd *frown*,
Since every Poet *knocks* me down;
Goodness waits always on the *Brave*;
Sure there's no Malice in the *Grace*:
Where have I done your Honours Wrong,
Either in Record, or in Song?
Alas, 'twas never in my *Will*,
And 'tis no Crime to have no *Skill*.

As he proceded to rehearse
The *Hardships* put upon his Verse,
And humbly crav'd both *Arthurs* Leaves
To pin his Fame upon their Sleeves;
Lo! and 'twas *wondrous* to behold
(And can't be without *Terror* told)
Of huge Size, a *Laureat* Wight
Came prancing in from *Stygian*-night:
The wooden *Machine* at the Door
Neigh'd thrice, in Homage to his Power:
His ghastly Brows with *Bays* were bound,
The product of *sulphureous* Ground;
His Eye-balls glow'd like red-hot *Bricks*,
And in his Hand a Quart of *Styx*;
Such *liquid* Flames, such *solid* Fire,
Many wou'd *fear*, but all admire.
The Bars, and Bolts, and Locks: Oh Wonder!
All of *themselves* burst quite asunder.
When he was to the Bed-side come,

The *Bard* was struck with *Horror* dumb;
The *gentle* Ghost advanc'd his Arm,
And told him, *Brother*, there's no harm;
Come, thy *dejected* Spirits chear,
Who sings of *Heroes* shou'd not *fear*.

He wipt his Face, and trembling said,
I was *surpris'd*, but not *afraid*;
Those verdant *Bays* that crown your Brows,
Your *Candour*, and your *Goodness* shows:
Poets are harmless, gay, and kind,
And shou'd be to each other blind;
Since you are than a *Son* of *Fame*,
Forgive my *Freedom*—What's your Name?
Tho' *scoundrel* Poets here harrass us,
You look like *Prætor* of *Parnassus*;
And since a Bard of *t'other* World,
More *Goodness* has you hether hurl'd,
And you to my *Assistance* come,
To supersede my *rigid* Doom,
You know, wise Sir—Yes, very well,
Quoth *Spright* that you're the *News* of Hell,
The *Scandal* of the *rhiming* Crew,
I *blush* to have been *rankt* with you;
My *Rhimes* with *me* were long since rotten,
And, but for *Arthurs*, quite forgotten;
I your *curs'd* Poems I *revive*,
And now again in *Scandal* live:
Pray what has poor *Habakkuk* done,
Thus to be lasht in your Lampoon?
His Character you shou'd have *spar'd*,
He was a *Prophet* not a *Bard*.
Job too does in your Poems *languish*
And suffer almost *hellish* Anguish.
Were he now *living*, and thy *Theme*,
He cou'd not help, but must *blaspheme*.

Sir, by your Favour, quoth the *Bard*,
Your *Censures* are unjust and hard;
I've done them *Honour*, as I think,
Or let my *Name* for ever stink.
Why that's most *certain*, quoth the Spright,
And thou'rt a *Coxcomb* by this Light,
So empty, sensless, and so dull,
Thou'rt every School-boy's Ridicule.
A damn'd *Reproach* to *Verse* and Prose,
As well as the *Gallenic* Dose.

What! saith the *Doctor*, in a Fury,
I no *Physician!*—I assure you
Diseases run from me affrighted;
My Skill's so great, that I am *Knighted*;
Such vast Discoveries I have made
Throughout the *Esculapian* Trade,
The *Cits* applaud, their *Wives* adore,
My numerous *Verse* and Medic Power.

Come, thou'rt a *Scoundrel*, quoth the Ghost;
Of *Wit* and *Cures* alike you boast;
Know I am *Mœvius*, that of old,
In *Thoughts* sublime and *Matter* bold,
Did every *versifying* Ass,
By a Bar's length at least, *surpass*;
And only am *out-done* by you
In lofty *Noise* and *Nonsense* too:
Then *Mœvius* tore his wither'd Bays,
And threw 'em in the *Doctor's* Face;
Who, being scar'd at such a Scene,
Has promis'd ne're to *Write* agen.

APPENDIXES

THE AUTHORSHIP OF *COMMENDATORY VERSES*

IN DETERMINING the authorship of the poems which are unsigned in *Commendatory Verses, Discommendatory Verses* and the various editions of Tom Brown's *Works* are useful. In the latter actual ascriptions are made; these, which in general run throughout all editions of Brown's *Works*, are given below; variations in specific editions are designated.

The poems in *Discommendatory Verses* are of value in this connection primarily as they match almost poem for poem the pieces in *Commendatory Verses*, and in doing so single out for attack the person believed to be the author. In this respect Brown's *Works* and *Discommendatory Verses* by and large agree with each other, though there are some striking and baffling differences. The evidence supporting the claims of the various authors is given below. The number before each title represents the poem's position in the collection.

THE EARL OF ANGLESEA

11. "Wholesome Advice to a City Knight." Assigned to Anglesea (the third earl) in various editions of Brown's *Works* and answered in *Discommendatory Verses* 11.

COL. HENRY BLOUNT

A Christ Church friend of Codrington's, killed at the battle of Schellenberg (1704), Blount is perhaps best known today for the commendatory poem he contributed to Garth's *Dispensary* (*Alumni Oxonienses*, ed. Joseph Foster, I, 141).

3. "To that Incomparable Panegyrist, the Author of the *Satyr upon Wit*." The early editions of Brown's *Works* attribute this simply

to " Coll. Bl[ount], but in the later editions Blount's name is given in full. It is answered by *Discommendatory Verses* 3.

DR. EDWARD BAYNARD

Baynard, a friend of Tom Brown's, had much of his practice at Bath, which may explain why he did not subscribe to the Dispensary project so ardently defended by Brown and his friends. Brown, twenty years Baynard's junior, frequently wrote him at Bath; one of his letters is given in Brown's *Works* (1720, I, 193-195, July 6, 1699). Brown also wrote a Latin elegy on Baynard's daughter Anne (*Works*, 1720, III, 275-276). Baynard himself wrote several poems, among them, *Health* (1719). (See B. Boyce, *Tom Brown*, p. 56, and *RES*, 14, 454, n. 2; William Munk, *Roll of the Royal College of Physicians*, London, 1861, I, 418-419.)

25. " Melancholy Reflections on the Deficiency of Useful Learning." Not printed in Brown's *Works*, but poems 29, 30, and 31 in *Discommendatory Verses* say it was written by " Dr. B[aynar]d." It is sometimes ascribed to Dr. Bernard (probably on the strength of the ascription in *Discommendatory Verses*), but that is most likely erroneous. The " Horoscope " of Garth's *Dispensary*, it is not probable that Bernard would line up with Garth, Drake, and the other Dispensarians in *Commendatory Verses*.

CHARLES BOYLE

4. " The Quack Corrected." Attributed in Brown's *Works* to the " Right Honourable Earl of [Orrery]"; Boyle became Earl of Orrery in 1703, after the publication of *Commendatory Verses*. *Discommendatory Verses* 4, which replies, is clearly aimed at Boyle. (For an account of Boyle's part in *Commendatory Verses* see above, pp. 22-24.)

NICHOLAS BRADY

22. " Epigram, Occasion'd by the Passage . . . that Reflects upon Mr. Tate." This poem is included in Volume I of Brown's *Works*, which suggests that Brown wrote it. However, *Discommendatory Verses* 25, which replies, is a biting retort directed at " B[ra]dy." Nicholas Brady, chaplain to William III, had translated the Psalms with Nahum Tate in 1696; William decreed that it might be used in place of the Sternhold and Hopkins version, a move that pleased many of the Whigs but annoyed the Tories (*DNB*, VI, 192-193). It is impossible to tell definitely whether Brown

or Brady wrote the piece in *Commendatory Verses*. It seems unlikely that Brady, the King's chaplain, would write against Blackmore, the King's physician, but, on the other hand, Blackmore's book, *Discommendatory Verses*, is unquestionably aimed at Brady. It is possible that Brady joined forces with the anti-Blackmoreans simply because he was offended by the slur on his friend Tate in the *Satyr against Wit*.

TOM BROWN

Brown's own poems in *Commendatory Verses* are printed in Volume I of his *Works*, where his authorship is signified on the title page of the volume only. (For a discussion of Brown's part in *Commendatory Verses* see above, pp. 37-41.)

14. "Occasion'd by the News that . . . *Job* was in the Press." Answered by *Discommendatory Verses* 14, which is clearly aimed at Brown. In the *Works*.

19. "Upon the Knighting of Sir R[ichard] Bl[ackmo]re." Answered by *Discommendatory Verses* 22, which is directed at Brown. In the *Works*.

20. "Upon Seeing King Arthur." Answered in *Discommendatory Verses* 23. In the *Works*.

21. "Upon Seeing a Man Light a Pipe." Answered by *Discommendatory Verses* 24. In the *Works*.

28. "To Elkanah Settle." *Discommendatory Verses* 35 answers this; the use of "I" in the reply suggests that it may have been written by Settle himself. *Commendatory Verses* 28 is in Brown's *Works*.

29. "To the Author of the Satyr against Wit." Answered by *Discommendatory Verses* 36. In the *Works*.

30. "On *Job* newly Travestied." Poems 37 and 38 in *Discommendatory Verses* answer this and are aimed at Brown. In the *Works*.

31. "To Sir R[ichard] Bl[ackmore]." Since this poem is printed in Volume I of Brown's *Works*, it would seem to be by Brown himself. However, *Discommendatory Verses* 39 implies that it was written by a cleric and one who had been attacked by Blackmore, presumably in the *Satyr against Wit*. The person who best fits this description is Dr. Smalwood (*Satyr against Wit*, pp. 6, 8, 14). It is probably Smalwood who is referred to in *Commendatory Verses* 7 and in the reply, *Discommendatory Verses* 7.

33. "On Sir R[ichard] Bl[ackmo]re's Noble Project." But *DV* 41 and 42 are aimed at Francis Manning. In the *Works*.

34. "To Sir R[ichard] Bl[ackmo]re, on the Two Wooden Horses." Answered by *Discommendatory Verses* 43 and 44; the former is said to be by "D—— P——" and is aimed at Brown. In the *Works*.

38. "Epigram upon *King Arthur*." Answered by *Discommendatory Verses* 49 and 50, which are directed at Brown. In the *Works*.

40. "An Epitome of . . . a *Satyr against Wit*." Answered by *Discommendatory Verses* 52. In the *Works*. (See also under *Brady* and *Sheffield*.)

WILLIAM BURNABY

A writer of late Restoration comedy, William Burnaby until recently has been confused with Charles Burnaby, a writer who apparently never existed. While at Oxford with Steele and Codrington he translated the *Satyricon* of Petronius; the inclusion of this version in the Modern Library is his only claim to recognition today. His plays were the product of his years in London, where he became known as one of the Wits at Will's. It has recently been suggested that Burnaby entered the Blackmore fight with his play, *The Reformed Wife* (April, 1700), in which the character of Bloodem is a satire on the City Bard (F. E. Budd, *Dramatic Works of William Burnaby*, London, 1931, pp. 51-52).

8. "To the Cheapside Knight." Attributed to Burnaby in Brown's *Works*, but the reply in *Discommendatory Verses* appears to name John Dennis as the author of *Commendatory Verses* 8. Either might have written the poem.

THOMAS CHEEK

37. "To . . . the Author of the *Satyr against Wit*." Some of the early editions of Brown's *Works* (1708, for one) attribute this poem (answered by *Discommendatory Verses* 48) to Cheek. He had already allied himself with the anti-Blackmoreans by contributing some verses to Garth's *Dispensary*. He was also a friend of Dennis's, and with him translated some of Voiture's letters in 1700 (*Dennis*, ed. Hooker, II, xiii, n. 10). However, there is an equally strong case for Thomas Creech, to whom most of the editions of Brown's *Works* ascribe this poem. Tom Brown had once written a poem in praise of Creech, "Upon Mr. Creech's

Translation of Lucretius " (*Works*, 1720, IV, 334) and had accused Dryden of attempting to ruin Creech's reputation as a translator (B. Boyce, *Tom Brown*, pp. 27-28). As a Fellow of All Souls, Creech had also made the fortunate acquaintance of Codrington, the instigator of *Commendatory Verses*, who gave Creech money from time to time; Creech dedicated his *Lucretius* to Codrington in 1694 (Harlow, *Christopher Codrington*, pp. 60-64). While it seems likely that Codrington would again have helped his charge by enlisting his services for *Commendatory Verses*, and that Creech would be willing to oblige his patron, certain facts about Creech's life make this improbable. Signs of insanity were evident by April, 1699, a malady which led to Creech's suicide in June, 1700, just a few months after the appearance of *Commendatory Verses*. It is possible that Creech had periods of complete sanity, of course, and it must be admitted that *Commendatory Verses* 37 is no more irrational than the other poems in the volume. (See also under *Mildmay*.)

KNIGHTLY CHETWOOD

17. " An Epigram on *Job* Travesty'd." Brown's *Works* gives Codrington as author, but the reply in *Discommendatory Verses* 19 names Chetwood; Codrington's biographer, V. T. Harlow, does not claim the poem for Codrington. A friend of Dryden's, Chetwood later became dean of Gloucester. It is possible that he wrote a poem for *Commendatory Verses*, which was sponsored by "Dryden's Crew" and directed at the Whig Blackmore (Chetwood had been James II's chaplain).

CHRISTOPHER CODRINGTON

The important part played by Codrington in the inception of *Commendatory Verses* has been described above (p. 48). He wrote the following poems for the volume:

1. " A Short and True History." In Brown's *Works*. *Discommendatory Verses* 1 is clearly a reply to this poem; even the title attacks Codrington, " A Short and True History of a Certain Captain-General." Harlow (*Christopher Codrington*, p. 94) agrees with this ascription. For years, however, this poem was attributed to Dr. James Drake, another writer who participated in the Blackmore quarrel. Dr. Johnson, for instance, quotes the opening lines as being by Drake (*Lives of the Poets*, ed. G. B. Hill, II, 236, n. 1), and Cibber and Shiels do likewise (*Lives of the*

Poets of Great Britain and Ireland . . . , 1753, V, 177). Since
Drake wrote the "Character of Mr. Tho. Brown, and His
Writings," which was prefixed to Brown's collected works, it
seems possible that the Codrington ascription may be inaccurate.

6. "An Equal Match." Answered by *Discommendatory Verses* 6.
In Brown's *Works*.

10. "A Modest Request to the Poetical Knight." Attributed to Codrington in Brown's *Works* and answered by *Discommendatory
Verses* 10, which is, however, directed at "H[en?]ly." It is
possible that the poem was written by Codrington's friend,
Anthony Henley, who, according to Harlow, *Christopher Codrington*, p. 95, wrote a poem for the volume. One of the Wits,
Henley was known for his generosity to struggling authors. To
him Garth dedicated his *Dispensary* and Purcell's opera, *Brutus
of Alba* (1696), was dedicated to Henley and Richard Norton,
another contributor to *Commendatory Verses* (*DNB*, XXV,
413-414).

15. "A Tale." Brown's *Works* attributes this to Codrington, but *Discommendatory Verses* 15 would suggest that it was by some
youth, probably a friend of Codrington's, who was misled.
Blackmore and his assistants seem to have been well informed
about Codrington's part in *Commendatory Verses*; for that
reason they may have been right in saying it was written by a
friend and not by Codrington himself.

16. "Upon the Character of Codron." This is attributed to Codrington
in Brown's *Works*, but Harlow (*Christopher Codrington*, p. 96)
says it is by William Walsh. It must be agreed that if Codrington wrote the poem extolling his own virtues he was not unduly
modest. However, if Walsh was the poet, he, too, is open to the
charge of vanity in such lines as: "*Voiture* and *Walsh* oft read
will never cloy." Poems 16, 17, and 18 in *Discommendatory
Verses*, the replies, seem to address not Codrington but a friend,
and so lend weight to the Walsh attribution. (See also above,
under *Chetwood*.)

THOMAS CREECH

(See above, under *Cheek*.)

JOHN DENNIS

(For Dennis's probable rôle in the collection see above, pp. 49-51.
He may have written *Commendatory Verses* 8. See above, under
Burnaby.)

DR. JAMES DRAKE

A strong Tory who attacked William III in his *History of the Last Parliament* (1702), Drake had been at Cambridge with Codrington. He entered the Collier controversy with his *Antient and Modern Stages Survey'd* (1699), which drew a compliment from Dryden in the Preface to the *Fables*. On this score and because he was in favor of the Dispensary Drake joined the attack on Blackmore. He also wrote a life of Tom Brown, which was prefixed to Brown's collected *Works*, as well as an inscription for Brown's monument.

32. "To Dr. Garth." In Brown's *Works* and answered by *Discommendatory Verses* 40, where Drake is named. (See also above, under *Codrington, CV* 1.)

SIR SAMUEL GARTH

Although Garth contributed but a single poem to *Commendatory Verses* he undoubtedly played an important part in the publication of the volume. For one thing, he was almost certainly responsible for the strong pro-Dispensarian views of the miscellany. (See above, pp. 48-49.)

5. "To the Merry Poetaster at Sadler's Hall." The early editions of Brown's *Works* ascribe this simply to "Dr. ***," but later Garth's name is given. Cushing accepts this (*Bulletin of the Johns Hopkins Hospital*, XVII, No. 178 [January, 1906], p. 5). Answered by *Discommendatory Verses* 5.

ANTHONY HENLEY

(For Henley's possible authorship of *Commendatory Verses* 10 see above, under *Codrington.*)

COL. JOHNSON

36. "To the Cheapside Quack." Although this poem is reprinted in Brown's *Works*, its author is usually not identified. In the *Last Works* (1708), however, a Col. Johnson is given as the poet. I have been unable to identify the writer; all that is known about him is that he was an admirer of Dr. Colbatch. *Commendatory Verses* 36 is answered by *Discommendatory Verses* 46 and 47.

FRANCIS MANNING

It is not surprising to find Manning's name in *Commendatory Verses*, for in 1700 he dedicated his *Generous Choice* to Codrington. In 1704 he dedicated the *History of Dion Cassius* to Charles Boyle, another leader in *Commendatory Verses*.

18. "To the Adventurous Knight of Cheapside." In Brown's *Works* and answered by *Discommendatory Verses*, poems 20 and 21; poem 20, however, says the author is a "captain." (See also above, under *Brown, 33*; and *Discommendatory Verses 5*.)

MILDMAY

26. "To the Canting Author of the Satyr against Wit." Most editions of Brown's *Works* state that this poem was written by "—— Mildmay," although the reply in *Discommendatory Verses 32* is directed at "C——k" (Cheek?) I am unable to identify any Mildmay who was mixed up, even remotely, in the quarrel.

LORD MORDAUNT

27. "Friendly Advice to Dr. Bl[ackmore]." In Brown's *Works* this is usually ascribed to "the Right Honourable the Lord ——." Perhaps the author was Lord Mordaunt, the son of the third Earl of Peterborough. Lord Mordaunt was, we know, one of Codrington's friends; Codrington left him a sum of money in his will (Harlow, *Christopher Codrington*, p. 219). Harlow says (p. 101) that Mordaunt contributed to *Commendatory Verses*, although I have been unable to find proof of such a connection. Poems 33 and 34 in *Discommendatory Verses*, the answers, imply that the writer was a member of the fashionable literary circle and had at one time fought the Moors unsuccessfully. Such a description actually fits the father better than the son, for Peterborough, later Swift's friend, had taken part in the fight against the Moors at Tangiers, in 1680. Furthermore, in "A New Year's Gift to the Secretary of the Muses" [1688?] Peterborough is called a "Railing Scribler" (reprinted in Brice Harris, "Robert Julian, Secretary to the Muses," in *ELH*, 10 [1943], 304). We know also that Peterborough was close to Codrington (Harlow, *op. cit.*, p. 100, *et passim*).

It is also possible that this poem was written by Sir Henry Sheeres (or Shears), who, Harlow claims (*op. cit.*, p. 232, n. 2), was one of the contributors. Sheeres, who died in 1710, was a military engineer and a friend of Pepys. Going to Tangiers in 1669, he remained there for fourteen years. When the place was abandoned in 1683, Sheeres superintended the blowing up of the Mole. He was a member of the Royal Society and wrote semi-technical treatises (which would seem to put him in a class with Sloane) and translated Polybius (1693) and Lucan (1711) (*DNB*, LII, 10-11). Poems 33 and 34 in *Discommendatory Verses* appear to be aimed at Sheeres, who was an engineer, defeated by the Moors, and a knight. On the other hand, the ascription in Brown's *Works* to "the Right Honourable the Lord ———" would hardly seem to fit.

RICHARD NORTON

A wealthy country gentleman of Southwick, Norton was known in his day as a staunch patron of the drama. His own attempt at dramatic composition was *Pausanius* (1696), but posterity remembers him as the person to whom Colley Cibber addressed his *Love's Last Shift*, one of the first of the sentimental comedies. Mrs. Behn's *Unfortunate Bride* (1698) was also dedicated to him. On August 10, 1708, John Dennis, probably another contributor to *Commendatory Verses*, wrote an effusive letter praising him as the savior of the stage (*Dennis*, ed. Hooker, II, xxviii, 392-393). Long considered queer (he was once accused of turning his chapel into a theater), Norton in his will left a large fortune to Parliament to be used for charitable purposes, but his will was set aside on the grounds that he was mentally unsound (John W. Dodds, *Thomas Southerne, Dramatist*, Yale Studies in English, New Haven, 1933, p. 19, n. 67).

39. "A Merry Ballad on the City Bard." Attributed to Norton in Brown's *Works* and answered by *Discommendatory Verses* 51, which attacks "N[orto]n." While most of the poems in *Commendatory Verses* are written in conventional heroic couplets, the poem by Norton is the only one which uses a different meter (alternating rhymes and alternating tetrameter and trimeter lines).

THE COUNTESS OF SANDWICH

Elizabeth Wilmot, the notorious Earl of Rochester's second daughter, was popularly credited with inheriting much of her father's famous wit; the indecency of her poem in *Commendatory Verses* shows that she had much in common with her father. She mar-

ried Edward Montague, third Earl of Sandwich, and died in
Paris on July 2, 1757. Not to be outdone, the editor of *Discommendatory Verses* also enlisted the services of the fair sex, in
39 and 40.

12. "To a Thrice Illustrious Quack." Answered by *Discommendatory
Verses* 12. In Brown's *Works*.

SIR CHARLES SEDLEY

A leader of the older group of Wits, Sedley is one of the better-known
contributors to *Commendatory Verses*. If it seems strange that
he should appear in such company, it should not be forgotten
that he did have a grudge against Blackmore, for he was ignored
in the *Satyr against Wit*.

2. "Upon the Author of the *Satyr against Wit*." In Brown's *Works*.
Discommendatory Verses 2, the reply, is addressed to "Sir
C[har]ls S[ed]ly," an ascription that V. de Sola Pinto accepts
(*Poetical and Dramatic Works of Sir Charles Sedley*, II, 252).
With a few variations, this poem is usually included in the
collected editions of Sedley's works.

SIR HENRY SHEERES

(For Sheeres's possible authorship of *CV* 27 see above, under *Lord
Mordaunt*.)

JOHN SHEFFIELD

Sheffield, the third Earl of Mulgrave, Marquis of Normanby, and Duke
of Buckingham, was well represented in the poetical miscellanies
of the day. A soldier of considerable standing, Sheffield became
a favorite of James II and profited handsomely by his enemy's
(Monmouth's) fall. After 1688 he became a leader of the Tories.
His *Essay on Poetry* and other pieces were widely read, and he
took further literary laurels on himself by being Dryden's patron
(*DNB*, LII, 13-15). Blackmore attempted to win his support in
the *Satyr against Wit* (pp. 9-10) but, failing, lashed out at him
in *Discommendatory Verses* 25 and 26. Sheffield again attacked
Blackmore in the "Election of a POET LAUREATE in 1719"
(*Works of His Grace the Duke of Buckingham*, Third Edition,
1740, I, 197):

"With a huge Mountain-load of Heroical Lumber
Which from TONSON to CURLL ev'ry Press had groan'd under:
Came BL[ACKMOR]E, and cryed, Look, all these are my Lays."

23. "A Story of a Greek Chevalier." Since this poem is printed in Volume I of Brown's *Works*, it would seem to be by Brown. However, Poems 26 and 27 in *Discommendatory Verses* are aimed at "Sh[effie]ld," who is a "L[or]d" and a "M[arqui]ss."

DR. SMALWOOD

(See above, under Brown, *CV* 31.)

DR. THOMAS SMITH

A fellow of Magdalen College, Oxford, Smith was one of the few there who refused to take the oath of allegiance to William and Mary, and as a result had to give up his fellowship. This alone would make him a fit contributor to the Tory-tinged *Commendatory Verses* (Harlow, *Christopher Codrington*, p. 95, n. 1).

9. "To the Indefatigable Rhimer." In Brown's *Works* and clearly answered in *Discommendatory Verses* 9. Harlow (*Christopher Codrington*, p. 95) accepts the ascription.

RICHARD STEELE

An acquaintance of Codrington's, Steele entered the war against Blackmore because of the latter's slur on Addison (whom Codrington also knew at Oxford) in the *Satyr against Wit* (p. 8). (See Harlow, *Christopher Codrington*, p. 56.)

7. "To the Mirrour of British Knighthood," which is also in Brown's *Works*. *Discommendatory Verses* 7 is the reply.

WILLIAM WALSH

Walsh, a friend of Dryden's, was well known by his contemporaries as a writer of short amorous pieces, and as the man who encouraged the young poet Pope. He knew Codrington in Paris, having met him there in 1698 (Harlow, *Christopher Codrington*, p. 86). (For his possible authorship of *Commendatory Verses* 16 see above, p. 138.)

THE UNIDENTIFIED POEMS

For a few poems there is little if any evidence of authorship:

13. "To Sir R[ichard] Bl[ackmore]." Unsigned in Brown's *Works*, IV. *Discommendatory Verses* 13, the reply, addresses a knight.

24. "To the Pious and Worthy Author." Not reprinted in Brown's *Works*. The poem is answered by *Discommendatory Verses* 28, where there is no clue to the author's identity.

35. "To a Famous Doctor and Poet." Answered by *Discommendatory Verses* 45. In Brown's *Works*, IV.

41. "A Lent-Entertainment." The poem added to the second issue of *Commendatory Verses*; not reprinted in Brown's *Works*.

CHRONOLOGY OF WORKS IN 1700 RELATED TO
COMMENDATORY VERSES

THE complexity of the *Commendatory Verses* quarrel is reflected in the various poems, letters, and other materials which are the heart of the fight. Most of these are simply marked " 1700," and since the order in which they appeared is of great importance in the present study, a suggested chronology is given below:

Satyr against Wit. Although 1700 is given on the title page of the first edition, it seems likely that it is inaccurate (see below, under " To Sir W. S—— "). Scott says that Luttrell's copy was marked November 23, 1699 (*Works of Dryden*, I, 421).

Dispensary, Fourth Edition. A reference to this in " To Sir W. S—— " (dated January 8) would put it before that time. It is also mentioned in the title of Drake's poem in *Commendatory Verses* 32, so that it obviously came out before the appearance of the volume.

Poetæ Britannici, by Samuel Cobb, is also referred to in " To Sir W. S——," although the Term Catalogue lists it under February.

" To Sir W. S—— " (*Works of . . . Voiture*, 1701 section, pp. 127-136) is dated January 8, which would seem to be accurate if November 23, 1699, is accepted as the date for the *Satyr against Wit*. It is unlikely that the " Jan. 8 " would mean 1701, for in the letter there is a clear reference to the projected *Commendatory Verses*, which did not come until March, 1700.

Paraphrase on the Book of Job. Constant allusions in *Commendatory Verses* to Blackmore's poem verify the fact that *Job* was either out or about to come out when the miscellany appeared. Actually, *Job* was advertised in the *London Gazette*, issue of February 29—March 4. In Steele's *Commendatory Verses* poem, " To the Mirrour of British

Knighthood," he addresses Blackmore as "Thou who . . . hast three Poems writ" (*Prince Arthur, King Arthur, Satyr against Wit*), data which demonstrate that *Job* had not yet been issued. However, the title of another poem in *Commendatory Verses* may hold the clue: "Occasion'd by the News that Sir R—— Bl——'s Paraphrase upon *Job* was in the Press." Since it was the custom for poems frequently to be circulated in manuscript before printing them, the Wits may have seen, or heard about, the forthcoming *Job*. The Advertisement at the end of *Commendatory Verses* states that *Job* is "Daily expected." Furthermore, while we do know that *Commendatory Verses* came out in March, we have no way of telling when the poems in that volume were written; Steele's, for instance, may have been several months before. Tom Brown's remark in "To Sir W. S—— " that a book lampooning Blackmore was in the wind would bear out such a conjecture.

Dryden's *Fables.* This work, which contains the two attacks on Blackmore, in "To My Honour'd Kinsman, John Driden" and the *Preface*, was advertised in the *Flying-Post*, March 5-7 (H. Macdonald, *John Dryden, a Bibliography*, p. 62).

Commendatory Verses was advertised in the *Post-Boy*, March 12-13 (*Dennis*, ed. Hooker, I, 448). See above, p. 37, n. 1.

"To a Physician in the Country" (in the *Works of . . . Voiture*, 1701 section, pp. 136-140) contains a fairly clear reference to *Discommendatory Verses*; in other words, it was probably written after the publication of *Commendatory Verses* and before the appearance of *Discommendatory Verses*.

Discommendatory Verses was dated April 6 by Luttrell (*Dennis*, ed. Hooker, I, 448) and was advertised in the *Flying-Post*, April 16-18.

Prologue to the *Pilgrim* was probably written between April 11 and April 29 (Macdonald, *op. cit.*, p. 135).

Homer and Virgil not to be compar'd. References to Dryden's funeral would put it after May 14.

New Session of the Poets, Daniel Kenrick's contribution to the quarrel, obviously comes after Dryden's death.

Epistle to Sr. Richard Blackmore is an answer to *A New Session of the Poets* and a defence of Blackmore. Luttrell's copy is marked November 1, but D. N. Smith's is November 19 (Macdonald, *op. cit.*, p. 299). It was listed in the *History of the Works of the Learned* for October.

Letters from the Dead. Ayloffe's letter contains a probable reference to the second edition of *Commendatory Verses*. The *Letters* were advertised in the *Post-Boy* for March 12, 1702.

INDEX OF NAMES OF PERSONS AND
TITLES OF WORKS